23-42

HAMILTON AND THE
NATIONAL DEBT

Problems in American Civilization

UNDER THE EDITORIAL DIRECTION OF
George Rogers Taylor

HAMILTON *and the* NATIONAL DEBT

EDITED WITH AN INTRODUCTION BY
George Rogers Taylor

Problems in American Civilization

READINGS SELECTED BY THE
DEPARTMENT OF AMERICAN STUDIES
AMHERST COLLEGE

D. C. HEATH AND COMPANY: Boston

INTRODUCTION

THE importance of national fiscal policy is attested by its significant role in many of the great crises of history. Merely to mention the Puritan, French, and American Revolutions is to bring to mind crucial issues involving budgets, debts, and taxes. Nor is it surprising to find that the most critical issue facing the new government of the United States during Washington's first administration was the financial one. This volume is devoted to the struggle arising out of Hamilton's proposals for dealing with the national debt.

In the narrow sense, public finance has to do with such technical matters as bonds (or stocks as they were called in Hamilton's time), interest rates, taxes, and sinking funds. But it is primarily with the larger implications of Hamilton's fiscal program that this volume is concerned — the philosophy underlying his measures and their impact on the social, economic, and political structure of society. However, to provide a reasonable acquaintance with the more technical aspects of the program and a necessary background for an understanding of the issues involved the first selection in this volume is from Shultz and Caine's *Financial Development of the United States*.

The three great state papers of Alexander Hamilton were his reports on *Publick Credit* (January 9, 1790), on *A National Bank* (December 13, 1790), and on *Manufactures* (December 5,

1791). These along with his recommendations for an excise, a mint, and a sinking fund comprehend the main items in his program for the new republic. The first of his reports, that on the *Publick Credit*, is, except for its more technical parts, reproduced in this volume. It contains the core of his program and for it he musters his most persuasive arguments. This report precipitated a great national contest out of which were born the Federalist and Anti-Federalist parties. After a prolonged struggle the recommendations for funding the federal debt and assuming the state debts received congressional approval. The companion measures, those for an excise, establishing a national bank, and establishing a sinking fund, were adopted against dogged, but on the whole less persistent, opposition.

The hotly contested battle precipitated by Hamilton's *Report on the Publick Credit* echoed within Washington's cabinet, in both Houses of Congress, in the public prints, and in drawing rooms and grog shops throughout the republic. The principals participating in this struggle were the giants of their day. On the one side were the Federalist leaders. At their head stood Hamilton, the leader who so dominated governmental policy during Washington's first administration that he functioned more nearly like a prime minister than has any other cabinet officer in all American history. To call the role of his chief supporters in Congress would be to name men like Rufus King of New York and Robert Morris of Pennsylvania, who were nationally known for their wealth and influence. Outstanding in the opposition was James Madison of Virginia. His supporters in Congress, men like William Maclay in the Senate and James Jackson in the House, were hardly as well known or of the same social standing as the Federalist leaders. Madison did, however, have powerful allies outside of Congress, men like the patriot Patrick Henry and the agrarian philosopher John Taylor of Caroline.

But it is after all not the public men who participated but the issues involved which give this contest its chief significance. How far should governmental policy sacrifice justice to expediency? Should fiscal measures be designed to favor agrarian or commercial interests? Or if it is desired to assist all, should this be accomplished through direct aid to commercial interests and thus by stimulating business, presumably benefit the whole country? And, finally, should financial measures be so designed as to strengthen the federal government or the state governments?

These are some of the fundamental problems posed by the great debate on Hamilton's debt program. They are sharply contested in the excerpts from Congressional debates and from pamphlets and newspapers which are reproduced in this volume. Sometimes, as will be seen, these disputes were not on the highest plane. The reader will soon discover that the process of policy determination in the early democracy involved, in addition to cold logic and high appeals to justice, not only sophistry and sentimentality but also some elements of low humor and name-calling — even as they do today. Nor were there lacking

indications that personal economic interests may have been then, as now, a factor of some importance in determining congressional attitudes toward legislation.

The major issues raised by the struggle over the funding program continue to be reflected in Congressional debates and newspaper headlines. High taxes and heavy war debts constantly pose the old problems of justice versus expediency. Fiscal proposals designed to benefit particular economic groups or to stimulate business activity still divide parties and create sectional interests. Even the problem of the effect of financial measures on the respective roles of the states and the federal government is fought over again in nearly every Congress.

It is hardly surprising, therefore, that neither the public nor historical scholars themselves have reached agreement in evaluating the fiscal program of the first Secretary of the Treasury. For the public this is reflected in their attitude toward the often-quoted statement that Andrew Mellon was the greatest Secretary of the Treasury since Alexander Hamilton. Some regard this as the highest praise; others feel that, whatever the merits of Andrew Mellon, this is conferring on him a doubtful distinction. So also, as illustrated by the last three items in this volume, do the historians differ in their judgment. Senator Henry Cabot Lodge, the conservative Republican senator from Massachusetts, views Hamilton's policies as favorably as did Fisher Ames, his predecessor from Boston more than a century earlier. On the basis of a careful examination of the original records a contemporary scholar, Irving Brant, emphasizes the role of the speculators and the liberal historian, Vernon Parrington, appraises these policies in a critical light which in 1790 would surely have pleased James Jackson, Hamilton's outspoken critic from the then remote state of Georgia.

[NOTE: The statements in The Clash of Issues on pp. xi–xii, below, are quoted from the following sources: Daniel Leonard, *Strictures and Observations upon the Three Executive Departments* (1792), ascribed to Leonard, reprinted in *Magazine of History*, Vol. 25, No. 4, p. 257; William Maclay, *Journal of William Maclay* (New York: D. Appleton and Company, 1890), p. 197; Oliver Wolcott, Sr., letter dated April 23, 1790, reproduced in George Gibbs, *Memoirs of Administrations of Washington and John Adams* (New York: William van Norden, 1846, 2 vols.), I, 45; James Jackson, speech, *Annals of Congress* (Gales and Seaton edition), II, 1692; Daniel Webster, speech delivered in the city of New York on March 10, 1831, in Lewis Henry Boutell, *Alexander Hamilton* (Chicago, 1890), p. 9; Frederick Scott Oliver, *Alexander Hamilton, An Essay on American Union* (New York: G. P. Putnam's Sons, 1918), p. 212; Irving Brant, *James Madison, Father of the Constitution, 1787–1800* (Indianapolis: The Bobbs-Merrill Company, 1950), p. 318; Vernon Louis Parrington, *Main Currents in American Thought* (New York: Harcourt, Brace and Company, 1930, 3 vols. in one), Book III, Part I, p. 300.]

CONTENTS

THE CLASH OF ISSUES

Hamilton's contemporaries

"The safety, dignity and prosperity of the United States have grown out of the systems he [Hamilton] has proposed. It is this important character who has taught us, and brought it home to the senses of the people at large, that public credit is an INESTIMABLE JEWEL. It is he who has taught us to derive an advantage from the public debt, by creating the means, out of the debt itself, to discharge it."

— DANIEL LEONARD
A Massachusetts Tory

"Hamilton, at the head of the speculators, with all the courtiers, are on one side. These I call the party who are actuated by interest. The opposition are governed by principle. But I fear in this case interest will outweigh principle."

— WILLIAM MACLAY
Senator from Pennsylvania

"Your observations respecting the public debts as essential to the existence of the national government are undoubtedly just, — there certainly cannot at present exist any other cement. The assumption of state debts is as necessary, and indeed more so, for the existence of the national government than those of any other description; if the state governments are to provide for their payment, these creditors will forever oppose all national provisions as inconsistent with their interest; which circumstances, together with the habits and pride of the local jurisdictions, will render the states very refractory. A rejection to provide for the state debts, which it seems has been done by a committee of Congress, if persisted in, I consider as an overthrow of the national government."

— OLIVER WOLCOTT, SR.
Lieutenant Governor of Connecticut

"So far will it be from producing the harmony the gentleman has supposed, that I think I can venture to prophesy it will occasion discord, and generate rancor against the Union. For if it benefits one part of the United States, it oppresses another. If it lulls the *Shays* of the North it will rouse the *Sullivans* of the South."

— JAMES JACKSON
Congressman from Georgia

"He [Hamilton] smote the rock of the national resources, and abundant streams of revenue gushed forth. He touched the dead corpse of Public Credit, and it sprung upon its feet."

— DANIEL WEBSTER

"Nothing of this work has ever been undone by succeeding generations of public servants, but has merely expanded and unfolded under the pressure of circumstances. . . . For his contrivance was like no human-made garment that is soon worn threadbare and outgrown, but rather like the bark of a tree, that from the very nature of its being is never inadequate, since it is a part of the living organism which it covers."

— FREDERICK SCOTT OLIVER

"Hamilton's men of enlightenment — those who were to bulwark the new government and cement the Union — had served an ultimatum: No assumption, no funding. They would get their profits, or let the nation go to pieces."

— IRVING BRANT

". . . no ethical gilding could quite conceal a certain ruthlessness of purpose; in practice justice became synonymous with expediency, and expediency was curiously like sheer Tory will to power."

— VERNON LOUIS PARRINGTON

William J. Shultz and M. R. Caine:
FEDERALIST FINANCE

THE victory of the Federalists in securing ratification of the Constitution assured them dominance, for a time at least, in all branches of the Federal Government. Finance was bound to be a major interest of this group of men who had set themselves to build the United States into a great commercial power. Before ever the Treasury Department was organized, Congress was discussing a revenue measure. A large proportion of the major items of legislation enacted during the twelve years spanned by Washington's and Adams's administrations was concerned with financial matters. Policies of national finance were laid down during these years that colored American financial history for three-quarters of a century. Only the Civil War era, the World War era, and the administration of Franklin D. Roosevelt can be compared to it for the rapid tempo of financial evolution. . . .

Funding and Assumption of the Old Public Debt

Federal assumption, by Constitutional provision, of Continental and Confederation debts was an obligation taken seriously by the Federalists, for its political as well as its financial aspects. Congress called upon Hamilton to prepare a report on the status of American debt outstanding and on the possibilities of its assumption by the new Federal Government. On January 9, 1790, Hamilton submitted his "Report on Public Credit," to Congress.

HAMILTON'S DEBT PLAN. The "Report on Public Credit" divided the public debt outstanding into three main categories — the Continental and Confederation foreign debt, the Continental and Confederation domestic debt, and the Revolutionary state indebtedness. The total, as of December 1789, was $77,000,000, divided as shown in the following table.

Hamilton's plan for disposing of this indebtedness was brief but comprehensive. The Federal Government should assume as its own obligation all items of this debt. In substitution for the various elements of the earlier debt, it should issue its own bonds, or "stock" as government debt certificates were then called. It should make such provision for the payment of interest on the federal debt created, and for its eventual retirement, that there would be no depreciation.

THE PUBLIC DEBT AS OF DECEMBER 1789

Foreign debt:

Principal (part not yet due, part already due and defaulted) ..	$10,070,307
Interest in default	1,640,072
Total foreign debt	$11,710,379

Domestic debt:

Principal (including registered debt, currency issues, army certificates, etc., reduced to specie value)	$27,383,918
Interest in default	13,030,168
Total domestic debt ...	$40,414,086

State debt:

Ascertained	$18,201,206
Estimated balance	6,798,794
Total state debt	$25,000,000
Total public debt	$77,124,465

Reprinted by permission from *Financial Development of the United States* by William J. Shultz and M. R. Caine, pp. 92, 96–103, 112–116. Copyright 1937 by Prentice-Hall, Inc., New York.

According to Hamilton's calculations, his funding and assumption policy would impose a debt burden of over $77,000,000 upon the new Federal Government. The prospect held no element of dismay for him. Governmental debt, he held, became a sort of circulating capital for the people. In his report to Congress he explained:

It is a well-known fact, that in countries in which the national debt is properly funded, and an object of established confidence, it answers most of the purposes of money. Transfers of stock, or public debt, are there equivalent to payments in specie; or, in other words, stock, in the principal transactions of business, passes current as specie. The same thing would, in all probability, happen here, under the like circumstances.

Funding of the existing scattered public debt under federal auspices, Hamilton argued, would serve three purposes: it would consolidate popular support of the Federal Government; it would establish a sound basis for the future credit of the government; and it would solve, at least for large-scale business transactions, the problem of currency shortage. He anticipated no difficulty in raising federal revenues sufficient to pay off this debt gradually and regularly.

Neither Congress nor the nation objected to Hamilton's proposal for the assumption of the outstanding foreign debt. Also, it was generally agreed that the Continental and Confederation domestic debt should be assumed and funded, although the terms of the assumption provoked considerable dispute. But the taking over of the state Revolutionary indebtedness was bitterly contested.

FUNDING OF THE DOMESTIC DEBT. Few, in or out of Congress, seriously objected to federal assumption of the principal of

Continental and Confederation debt. But was it necessary to pay interest as well as principal? Long arrearages had cumulated the interest until it totaled almost half as much as the principal. Mere payment of the principal would be a windfall to the many holders of the old Continental and Confederation obligations who had long since surrendered all but a bare speculative hope of ever being paid. Why pile an additional $13,000,000 of interest arrearages on the enormous total of federal debt already in prospect? Hamilton's position on this issue was clear and curt. During the next few years, the United States would be a heavy borrower. Its credit must be above reproach. It dare not awaken the suspicion that it would ever trade on its weakness to countenance gratuitous loans. An overwhelming majority of Congress agreed with the Secretary's view.

A second and more bitterly contested issue intruded upon the general question of federal funding of the old domestic debt. In many if not most cases, the original recipients of Continental and Confederation certificates of indebtedness and bills of credit had disposed of their holdings at greatly depreciated prices. From 1787 on, there was a growing speculative buying and selling of these instruments, on the prospect that they might be redeemed by the new Federal Government. Speculation reached its climax while the Redemption Act was under debate. To redeem this debt in 1790 at its full specie value would present a rich bonus to the speculators. It would not benefit the original creditors of the Continental and Confederation Governments who had sold out. Why not, proposed some members of Congress, pay one-half the value of Continental and Confederation certificates of indebtedness to the original recipients of these instruments, as shown by the record books still in existence, and one-half to the present holders?

To Hamilton, this problem was a Gordian knot, incapable of untanglement, that could be severed only by a clean, direct cut. The half-and-half solution would at best work only a fractional justice. There was no guarantee that it represented a fair division between original and ultimate holders. It took no cognizance of the rights of intermediate holders. It could not be applied in the case of bills of credit and other items of the public debt for which there were no records of original issue. Furthermore, and most important in Hamilton's eyes, it conflicted with his policy of establishing the federal debt as a homogeneous, negotiable body of intangible wealth. As he told Congress:

The impolicy of a discrimination results from two considerations. One, that it proceeds upon a principle destructive of that quality of the public debt . . . which is essential to its capacity for answering the purposes of money — that is, the security of transfer; the other that, as well on this account, as because it includes a breach of faith, it renders property in the funds less valuable; consequently, induces lenders to demand a higher premium for what they lend, and produces every other inconvenience of a bad state of public credit.

Partly won over by Hamilton's logic, partly in deference to Washington's approval, partly influenced in their individual votes by the circumstance that many were speculative holders of the old debt, the members of the House and the Senate sustained Hamilton's policy. Current holders of the public debt were to be paid in full.

The Funding Act of 1790, provided for the issue of federal bonds sufficient to cover all exchanges of the old Continental and Confederation domestic debt. Three types of securities were authorized. Two-thirds of the value of each exchange was to be made in bonds bearing six per cent interest from their inception; the remaining third was to be made in bonds on which interest was deferred for ten years. Indents and other evidences of accrued interest were to be funded by three per cent bonds.

ASSUMPTION OF THE STATE DEBT. Hamilton's desire for federal assumption of state Revolutionary debts was dictated by two considerations — one political, the other financial. He wanted to use the strength of federal credit to wean the loyalties of the people from the state governments to the new Federal Government. In his report to Congress he argued:

If all the public creditors receive their dues from one source, distributed with an equal hand, their interest will be the same; and having the same interest, they will unite in the support of the fiscal arrangements of the Government.

Moreover, he was heartily willing to see an additional $25,000,000 of federal securities issued, feeling as he did that every dollar of federal debt represented circulating wealth available for the promotion of trade and industry. Behind these practical arguments lay the general thought that the state debts had been incurred in the struggle for liberty, and that the Federal Government was morally responsible for all the costs of that struggle.

A strong group in Congress opposed federal assumption of the state Revolutionary debt, both in its general principle and in its detailed provisions. Representatives of the southern states argued that since their states had relatively small debts, federal assumption would work unjustly. Gallatin, then in the House of Representatives, further argued that a careful checking of accounts, and a writing off of amounts owed, for one reason or another, by the states to the Continental and Confederation Governments, would reduce the total of state debt to be assumed to $11,600,000.

Hamilton as usual had his way, but only by negotiating a trade with the representatives of the southern states. In exchange for their votes on this feature of the Funding Act, the national capitol would be located in a "federal district" in territory set aside by Virginia and Maryland. The measure finally passed provided for a $21,500,000 federal bond issue to fund the state debts.[1] In most cases, the bonds were to be exchanged against outstanding items of state debt — paper currency issues calculated at specie value, certificates of indebtedness, warrants of all kinds, pay notes, various evidences of claims. The state governments themselves received bonds for such part of their debt as they had retired and for balances due them on their financial transactions with the Continental and Confederation Governments. No set-off was made for balances owed by the states.

These federal funding bonds were divided into three classes. Each creditor received four-ninths of his payment in bonds bearing six per cent interest, payable from the date of issue. Another two-ninths of each payment was made in bonds that were interest-free for ten years, then paid six per cent. The bonds

of the final one-third payment bore three per cent interest, payable from the date of issue.

PROVISIONS FOR DEBT SERVICE. The keystone of Hamilton's public debt policy was unqualified maintenance of the national credit. Never again should the government's ability to fulfill its foreign domestic debt obligations be questioned. Interest payments must be met regularly and fully, and there must be assurance from the very beginning that they would be so met. If possible, the bonds of the national debt should be sustained at a premium; under no circumstances should they be allowed to stay at a serious discount for any period of time. The Funding Act of 1790 and several subsequent measures provided the machinery for effecting Hamilton's intent.

With respect to their redemption, the bonds issued under the Act of 1790 were of novel character. In any year the government might pay part of the principal of all outstanding bonds. Such repayment in any one year might not exceed $8.00 on $100.

To assure holders of the new federal debt issues that interest payments on their holdings would continue, the Act of 1790 earmarked certain items of federal revenue to this purpose. The government was to be allowed $600,000 from the annual customs and tonnage receipts for its current expenses; the balance would be set aside for interest payment on the foreign debt. Later, during the first session of Congress, a special revenue measure was passed levying additional taxes, the receipts of which were earmarked to interest payments on the new domestic debt.

Finally, the Act of 1790 provided that at the end of each fiscal year any surplus standing to the credit of the Federal Government should be paid into a special

---

[1] As it turned out, this was an over-generous estimate. The total value of state indebtedness eventually submitted for exchange and of state balances reimbursed was $18,271,786.

fund managed by a board composed of the President, the Chief Justice of the Supreme Court, the Secretary of State, the Secretary of the Treasury, and the Attorney General. This board would buy up on the open market any federal debt issues that had fallen below par. The purpose of this arrangement was not so much to provide for retirement of the federal debt as to maintain its market value and so enhance the national credit. If the values in the Purchase Fund did not suffice to sustain the outstanding issues, the President was further empowered to borrow $2,000,000 at not more than five per cent interest and apply the sum to Purchase Fund operations. In 1792 it was provided that interest on any parts of the debt actually retired through the Purchase Fund should be continued and paid into the Fund.

Little thought was given at first to the retirement of the federal debt. The Funding Act of 1790 provided only that the proceeds from the sale of western lands should be devoted to debt redemption. The Purchase Fund created at the same time was viewed rather as a means of maintaining the market price of the debt than as an agency for its retirement. Additional items of income were voted to the Purchase Fund in 1792 and 1795, and these tended to make it truly a sinking fund to encompass the retirement of the debt. The Federal Government was receiving more in dividends on its holdings of United States Bank stock than the interest it was paying to the Bank on its loans. This excess was now voted to the Fund. Furthermore, an annual appropriation sufficient, together with the Fund's other income, to buy in one-fiftieth of the six per cent bonds outstanding, was appropriated to the Fund from the general revenues of the government. . . .

Federal Debt Policy

When Alexander Hamilton saddled the Federal Government with a $75,000,000 debt, he anticipated that this obligation would be steadily, if slowly, retired out of surpluses of receipts over expenditures. The expenditures of the government proved larger than his expectations, its revenues lower. Even with a revenue system expanded far beyond Hamilton's original intentions, the Federal Government could not consistently balance its budgets during its first decade. Much less could it make any progress towards reducing the total of its debt. Indeed, by January 1, 1801 the national debt was $7,500,000 greater than it had been ten years earlier. Hamilton's funding and assumption program, instead of ending the public debt problem, merely substituted a new problem for an old one. This new problem continued to plague the administrations of Washington and Adams.

SHORT-TERM DEBT. The new Federal Government inaugurated its existence by borrowing. During September, October, and December of 1789, the Bank of New York and the Bank of North America extended $170,000 to cover the first instalments on the salaries of the President, the Vice President, and the members of Congress, and for certain other vital expenses. These loans were repaid during the following year, but they were replaced by other borrowings. Both banks continued to lend to the government until 1793.

In December 1791 the Bank of the United States opened, and the Federal Government had a new source for temporary borrowings. A first loan for $400,000 was made in May 1792. By the close of the year, the government owed the new bank and the two older banks $2,500,000. By 1795 the total of temporary borrowings from the Bank of the United States was $4,500,000; by 1796 it was $6,200,000. In indebting itself heavily to the Bank of the United States, the Federal Government was obviously misusing its privileges and seriously endangering the Bank's stability. In 1796 and 1797, the government sold part of its Bank stock holdings, floated a long-term loan, and used the funds obtained to reduce its debt to the Bank below $4,000,000.

LONG-TERM DEBT. The first, and for several years the only, long-term debt issues of the Federal Government were the six per cent stock, the three per cent stock, and the "deferred" stock issued to fund the old public debt. By 1796, when the major part of the debt funding operations was completed, $41,700,000 of the six per cent stock, $18,900,000 of the three per cents, and $14,650,000 of the deferred stock, was outstanding.

Hamilton was desperately anxious that this federal stock should maintain its value on the market. The Purchase Fund, already described, was part of his plan for maintaining the price of the stock. Its operations were not ineffective. During the first quarter of 1791, the six per cent stock had sold off to 82. The three per cents and the deferred issues were selling at 42. A year later the six per cents had risen to 125 and the others to 75. By December 1795 the Fund had expended $1,600,000 to purchase $2,300,000 par value of the outstanding stock.

In 1795, to provide for the consistent retirement of the long-term debt, the Purchase Fund was developed into the Sinking Fund. At first the revenues dedicated to it were insufficient to buy up the prescribed annual quota of the outstanding debt, and part of the federal borrowings from the Bank of the United

States were applied to the Sinking Fund. During the second half of the decade, the Fund had sufficient revenue to fulfill its purpose — the annual reduction of the principal of the six per cent debt by onefiftieth of its original total. This pitifully slow rate of retirement was insufficient to maintain the market for any of the government issues, however, and they fell off badly.

In 1795 the government made the first increase in its domestic debt. As subsequently described, it issued and turned over to the French Government $1,850,000 in 5½ per cent stock and $176,000 in 4½ per cent stock, as final settlement of the American Revolutionary debt to France. A year later the government attempted to sell a six per cent $5,000,000 issue for the purpose of clearing its indebtedness to the Bank of the United States. But the market was saturated with the old issues, which, since the Purchase Fund had ceased its forceful operations, had fallen to sharp discounts. To the offer of the new issue there was no response, and after several months only $80,000, at oneeighth discount, had been subscribed.

Three domestic loans were floated in 1798, this time with more success. The first of these loans, a 6 per cent issue, was to provide the navy needed to combat the Barbary pirates who were preying on American shipping in the Mediterranean. Subscriptions at par totaled slightly over $700,000. Later in the year, when war with France seemed imminent, the government decided to build up a treasury reserve adequate for emergencies, and a $5,000,000, 8 per cent, fifteen-year loan was floated. The interest offered was above the market rate, the credit of the government by this time was considered sound, and the entire issue was readily marketed at par. Another $1,500,000 issue, on the same terms, for the purpose of covering anticipated current deficits, was taken up at a 5¾ per cent premium.

THE FOREIGN DEBT. The final element of the public debt was the $12,000,000 owed to France and to Holland. Accrued interest for several years and parts of the principal of these loans were in default in 1790, but most of the instalments on the principal had not yet fallen due. The Dutch were quite willing to make a new series of loans to clear the old defaults, and in 1790 a $1,200,000 loan was negotiated. Seven others followed in the course of the next four years. Dutch loans during the 1790's totaled $9,400,000.

The terms of these loans were exceptionally liberal. Their repayment was not to begin until 1802, and was then to proceed serially. Interest rates varied between 4 and 5 per cent, with "commissions" or discounts on the occasion of the making of the loans between 3½ and 5½ per cent.

Most of the funds received from these Dutch loans were used exclusively for service on the preexisting foreign debt; $3,000,000 was employed to purchase domestic debt issues. By the second half of the decade, the Federal Government was using its own funds to meet foreign debt obligations as they came due. By the close of Adams's administration nearly $2,000,000 had been repaid to the Dutch.

Slightly more than $2,000,000 of the old Revolutionary debt to France was still outstanding in 1789. Negotiations on the conversion of this item dragged. Finally, in 1795, the revolutionary French government agreed to accept American bonds, payable in dollars, and bearing interest at 4½ and 5½ per cent, for the amount owed. Two issues of bonds, re-

deemable between 1807 and 1815, were authorized to effect the transaction. Thus the French debt was merged with the domestic long-term debt.

Critique of Federalist Fiscal Policy

In the main, the Federalists achieved their ambition — the creation of a central government strong enough to weld a people into a nation, strong enough to foster a national industry and commerce, strong enough to command the respect of the Old World powers. Their contemporaries questioned whether they did not force their policy at too fast a pace, in view of existing resources and development of the country. The cost of their accomplishments, reflected in the current accounts and balance sheets of the Federal Government, certainly lent color to the arguments of their Republican critics.

At the close of the Federalist era of domination, the Federal Government was devoting over 55 per cent of its expenditures to the army and navy. Another 30 per cent went to interest on the national debt. Heavier interest payments were in immediate prospect since payments on the deferred debt were to begin in 1801. Even without taking into account appropriations for the retirement of the national debt, the Federalists had saddled the government with a military and interest budget that threatened to topple the structure of federal finances. Despite the addition of tax after tax to the revenue system, the Federal Government's receipts through the decade of the 90's were barely able to cling to the skirts of its expenditures. In 1800 the delicate equilibrium was ruptured. The outgoing Adams administration had resort to the dangerous expedient of incurring long-term loans to cover current deficits.

Disaster did not lie ahead. The Federalists' political and fiscal policies had sowed fertile seed for corrective reaction. Under the leadership of Thomas Jefferson, the reaction achieved political solidarity. Organized as the Republican Party, it made steady political gains throughout the 90's. Aided by dissension within the Federalist camp, it was practically assured of victory in 1800. The magnificent over-ambitions of Alexander Hamilton would be corrected by the equally magnificent caution of Albert Gallatin.

Alexander Hamilton:
REPORT ON PUBLIC CREDIT

Treasury Department, Jan. 9, 1790.

THE Secretary of the Treasury, in obedience to the resolution of the House of Representatives, of the twenty-first day of September last, has, during the recess of Congress, applied himself to the consideration of a proper plan for the support of the Public Credit, with all the attention which was due to the authority of the House, and to the magnitude of the object.

In the discharge of this duty, he has felt, in no small degree, the anxieties which naturally flow from a just estimate of the difficulty of the task, from a well-founded diffidence of his own qualifications for executing it with success, and from a deep and solemn conviction of the momentous nature of the truth contained in the resolution under which his investigations have been conducted, "That an *adequate* provision for the support of the Public Credit is a matter of high importance to the honour and prosperity of the United States."

With an ardent desire that his well-meant endeavours may be conducive to the real advantage of the nation; and with the utmost deference to the superior judgment of the House, he now respectfully submits the result of his inquiries and reflections, to their indulgent construction.

In the opinion of the Secretary, the wisdom of the House, in giving their explicit sanction to the proposition which has been stated, cannot but be applauded by all, who will seriously consider, and trace through their obvious consequences, these plain and undeniable truths:

That exigencies are to be expected to occur, in the affairs of nations, in which there will be a necessity for borrowing:

That loans in times of public danger, especially from foreign war, are found an indispensable resource, even to the wealthiest of them:

And that in a country, which, like this, is possessed of little active wealth, or in other words, little monied capital, the necessity for that resource must, in such emergencies, be proportionably urgent.

And as on the one hand, the necessity for borrowing in particular emergencies cannot be doubted, so on the other, it is equally evident, that to be able to borrow upon *good terms*, it is essential that the credit of a nation should be well established.

For when the credit of a country is in any degree questionable, it never fails to give an extravagant premium, in one shape or another, upon all the loans it has occasion to make. Nor does the evil end here; the same disadvantage must be sustained upon whatever is to be bought on terms of future payment.

From this constant necessity of *borrowing* and *buying dear*, it is easy to conceive how immensely the expenses of a nation, in a course of time, will be augmented by an unsound state of the public credit.

To attempt to enumerate the complicated variety of mischiefs in the whole system of the social economy, which proceed from a neglect of the maxims that uphold public credit, and justify the solicitude manifested by the House on this point, would be an improper intrusion on their time and patience.

In so strong a light, nevertheless, do they appear to the Secretary, that on their due observance at the present critical juncture, materially depends, in his judgment, the individual and aggregate prosperity of the citizens of the United States: their relief from the embarrassments they now experience; their character as a people; the cause of good government.

If the maintenance of public credit, then, be truly so important, the next inquiry which suggests itself is, by what means it is to be effected: — The ready answer to which question is, by good faith, by a punctual performance of contracts. States, like individuals, who observe their engagements, are respected and trusted: while the reverse is the fate of those, who pursue an opposite conduct.

Every breach of the public engagements, whether from choice or necessity, is in different degrees hurtful to public credit. When such a necessity does truly exist, the evils of it are only to be palliated by a scrupulous attention on the part of the government, to carry the violation no further than the necessity absolutely requires, and to manifest, if the nature of the case admit of it, a sincere disposition to make reparation, whenever circumstances shall permit. But with every possible mitigation, credit must suffer, and numerous mischiefs ensue. It is therefore highly important, when an appearance of necessity seems to press upon the public councils, that they should examine well its reality, and be perfectly assured, that there is no method of escaping from it, before they yield to its suggestions. For though it cannot safely be affirmed, that occasions have never existed, or may not exist, in which violations of the public faith, in this respect, are inevitable; yet there is great reason to believe, that they exist far less frequently than precedents indicate; and are oftenest either pretended through levity, or want of firmness, or supposed through want of knowledge. Expedients might often have been devised to effect, consistently with good faith, what has been done in contravention of it. Those who are most commonly creditors of a nation, are, generally speaking, enlightened men; and there are signal examples to warrant a conclusion, that when a candid and fair appeal is made to them, they will understand their true interest too well to refuse their concurrence in such modifications of their claims, as any real necessity may demand.

While the observance of that good faith, which is the basis of public credit,

is recommended by the strongest inducements of political expediency, it is enforced by considerations of still greater
authority. There are arguments for it,
which rest on the immutable principles
of moral obligation: And in proportion
as the mind is disposed to contemplate,
in the order of Providence, an intimate
connexion between public virtue and
public happiness, will be its repugnancy
to a violation of those principles.

This reflection derives additional
strength from the nature of the debt of
the United States. It was the price of
liberty. The faith of America has been
repeatedly pledged for it, and with
solemnities, that give peculiar force to
the obligation. There is indeed reason to
regret that it has not hitherto been kept;
that the necessities of the war, conspiring
with inexperience in the subjects of
finance, produced direct infractions; and
that the subsequent period has been a
continued scene of negative violation, or
non-compliance. But a diminution of
this regret arises from the reflection, that
the last seven years have exhibited an
earnest and uniform effort, on the part
of the government of the union, to re-
trieve the national credit, by doing justice to the creditors of the nation; and
that the embarrassments of a defective
constitution, which defeated this laud-
able effort, have ceased.

From this evidence of a favourable
disposition, given by the former government, the institution of a new one,
clothed with powers competent to calling forth the resources of the community,
has excited correspondent expectations.
A general belief accordingly prevails,
that the credit of the United States will
quickly be established on the firm foundation of an effectual provision for the
existing debt. The influence, which this
has had at home, is witnessed by the

rapid increase that has taken place in
the market-value of the public securities.
From January to November, they rose
thirty-three and a third per cent and
from that period to this time, they have
risen fifty per cent more. And the intelligence from abroad announces effects proportionably favourable to our national
credit and consequence.

It cannot but merit particular attention, that among ourselves the most enlightened friends of good government
are those, whose expectations are the
highest.

To justify and preserve their confidence; to promote the increasing respect-
ability of the American name; to answer
the calls of justice; to restore landed
property to its due value; to furnish new
resources both to agriculture and commerce; to cement more closely the union
of the states; to add to their security
against foreign attack; to establish public order on the basis of an upright and
liberal policy — These are the great and
invaluable ends to be secured, by a
proper and adequate provision, at the
present period, for the support of public
credit.

To this provision we are invited, not
only by the general considerations, which
have been noticed, but by others of a
more particular nature. It will procure
to every class of the community some
important advantages, and remove some
no less important disadvantages.

The advantage to the public creditors
from the increased value of that part of
their property which constitutes the
public debt, needs no explanation.

But there is a consequence of this,
less obvious, though not less true, in
which every other citizen is interested.
It is a well-known fact, that in countries
in which the national debt is properly
funded, and an object of established con-

fidence, it answers most of the purposes of money. Transfers of stock or public debt, are there equivalent to payments in specie; or in other words, stock, in the principal transactions of business, passes current as specie. The same thing would, in all probability, happen here, under the like circumstances.

The benefits of this are various and obvious.

First. Trade is extended by it; because there is a larger capital to carry it on, and the merchant can at the same time afford to trade for smaller profits; as his stock, which when unemployed, brings him in an interest from the government, serves him also as money, when he has a call for it in his commercial operations.

Secondly. Agriculture and manufactures are also promoted by it; for the like reason, that more capital can be commanded to be employed in both; and because the merchant, whose enterprise in foreign trade gives to them activity and extension, has greater means for enterprise.

Thirdly. The interest of money will be lowered by it; for this is always in a ratio to the quantity of money, and to the quickness of circulation. This circumstance will enable both the public and individuals to borrow on easier and cheaper terms.

And from the combination of these effects, additional aids will be furnished to labour, to industry, and to arts of every kind.

But these good effects of a public debt are only to be looked for, when, by being well funded, it has acquired an *adequate* and *stable* value. Till then, it has rather a contrary tendency. The fluctuation and insecurity incident to it in an unfunded state, render it a mere commodity, and a precarious one. As such, being only an object of occasional and particular speculation, all the money applied to it, is so much diverted from the more useful channels of circulation, for which the thing itself affords no substitute: So that, in fact, one serious inconvenience of an unfunded debt is, that it contributes to the scarcity of money.

This distinction, which has been little, if at all, attended to, is of the greatest moment. It involves a question immediately interesting to every part of the community; which is no other than this —Whether the public debt, by a provision for it on true principles, shall be rendered a *substitute* for money; or whether, by being left as it is, or by being provided for in such a manner as will wound those principles, and destroy confidence, it shall be suffered to continue, as it is, a pernicious drain of our cash from the channels of productive industry?

The effect which the funding of the public debt, on right principles, would have upon landed property, is one of the circumstances attending such an arrangement, which has been least adverted to, though it deserves the most particular attention.

The present depreciated state of that species of property is a serious calamity. The value of cultivated lands, in most of the states, has fallen since the revolution from 25 to 50 per cent. In those furthest south, the decrease is still more considerable. Indeed, if the representations, continually received from that quarter, may be credited, lands there will command no price which may not be deemed an almost total sacrifice.

This decrease in the value of lands, ought, in a great measure, to be attributed to the scarcity of money. — Consequently, whatever produces an augmentation of the monied capital of the country, must have a proportional effect in raising that value. The beneficial tendency of a funded debt, in this respect, has been manifested by the most decisive experience in Great Britain.

The proprietors of lands would not only feel the benefit of this increase in the value of their property, and of a more prompt and better sale, when they had occasion to sell; but the necessity of selling would be itself greatly diminished. As the same cause would contribute to the facility of loans, there is reason to believe that such of them as are indebted would be able, through that resource, to satisfy their more urgent creditors.

It ought not however to be expected, that the advantages, described as likely to result from funding the public debt, would be instantaneous. It might require some time to bring the value of stock to its natural level, and to attach to it that fixed confidence, which is necessary to its quality as money. Yet the late rapid rise of the public securities encourages an expectation, that the progress of stock to the desirable point, will be much more expeditious than could have been foreseen. And as in the mean time it will be increasing in value, there is room to conclude, that it will, from the outset, answer many of the purposes in contemplation. Particularly it seems to be probable, that from creditors, who are not themselves necessitous, it will early meet with a ready reception in payment of debts, at its current price.

Having now taken a concise view of the inducements to a proper provision for the public debt, the next inquiry which presents itself is, what ought to be the nature of such a provision? This requires some preliminary discussions.

It is agreed on all hands, that that part of the debt which has been contracted abroad, and is denominated the foreign debt, ought to be provided for, according to the precise terms of the contracts relating to it. The discussions which can arise, therefore, will have reference essentially to the domestic part of it, or to that which has been contracted at home. It is to be regretted, that there is not the same unanimity of sentiment on this part, as on the other.

The Secretary has too much deference for the opinions of every part of the community, not to have observed one, which has, more than once, made its appearance in the public prints, and which is occasionally to be met with in conversation. It involves this question, whether a discrimination ought not to be made between original holders of the public securities, and present possessors, by purchase? Those who advocate a discrimination, are for making a full provision for the securities of the former, at their nominal value; but contend, that the latter ought to receive no more than the cost to them, and the interest: And the idea is sometimes suggested of making good the difference to the primitive possessor.

In favour of this scheme, it is alleged, that it would be unreasonable to pay twenty shillings in the pound, to one who had not given more for it than three or four. And it is added, that it would be hard to aggravate the misfortune of the first owner, who, probably through necessity, parted with his property at so great a loss, by obliging him to contribute to the profit of the person who had speculated on his distresses.

The Secretary, after the most mature reflection on the force of this argument, is induced to reject the doctrine it contains, as equally unjust and impolitic; as highly injurious, even to the original holders of public securities; as ruinous to public credit.

It is inconsistent with justice, because, in the first place, it is a breach of contract; a violation of the rights of a fair purchaser.

The nature of the contract in its origin, is, that the public will pay the sum expressed in the security, to the first holder, or his *assignee*. The *intent* in making the security assignable, is, that the proprietor may be able to make use of his property, by selling it for as much as it *may be worth in the market*, and that the buyer may be *safe* in the purchase.

Every buyer, therefore, stands exactly in the place of the seller — has the same right with him to the identical sum expressed in the security; and having acquired that right by fair purchase, and in conformity to the original *agreement* and *intention* of the government, his claim cannot be disputed without manifest injustice.

That he is to be considered as a fair purchaser, results from this: Whatever necessity the seller may have been under, was occasioned by the government, in not making a proper provision for its debts. The buyer had no agency in it, and therefore ought not to suffer. He is not even chargeable with having taken an undue advantage: He paid what the commodity was worth in the market, and took the risks of reimbursement upon himself. He of course gave a fair equivalent, and ought to reap the benefit of his hazard; a hazard which was far from inconsiderable, and which, perhaps, turned on little less than a revolution in government.

That the case of those who parted with their securities from necessity, is a hard one, cannot be denied. But whatever complaint of injury, or claim of redress they may have, respects the government solely. They have not only nothing to object to the persons who relieved their necessities by giving them the current price of their property, but they are even under an implied condition to contribute to the reimbursement of those persons. They knew, that by the terms of the contract with themselves, the public were bound to pay to those to whom they should convey their title, the sums stipulated to be paid to them; and that, as citizens of the United States, they were to bear their proportion of the contribution for that purpose. This, by the act of assignment, they tacitly engage to do; and if they had an option, they could not, with integrity or good faith, refuse to do it, without the consent of those to whom they sold.

But though many of the original holders sold from necessity, it does not follow, that this was the case with all of them. It may well be supposed, that some of them did it either through want of confidence in an eventual provision, or from the allurements of some profitable speculation. How shall these different classes be discriminated from each other? How shall it be ascertained, in any case, that the money, which the original holder obtained for his security, was not more beneficial to him, than if he had held it to the present time, to avail himself of the provision which shall be made? How shall it be known, whether, if the purchaser had employed his money in some other way, he would not be in a better situation, than by having applied it in the purchase of securities, though he should now receive their full amount? And if neither of these things can be known, how shall it be determined whether a discrimination, independent of the breach of contract, would not do a

real injury to purchasers; and if it included a compensation to the primitive
proprietors, would not give them an
advantage, to which they had no equitable pretension?

It may well be imagined, also, that
there are not wanting instances, in which
individuals, urged by a present necessity,
parted with the securities received by
them from the public, and shortly after
replaced them with others, as an indemnity for their first loss. Shall they be deprived of the indemnity which they have
endeavoured to secure by so provident
an arrangement?

Questions of this sort, on a close in-
spection, multiply themselves without
end, and demonstrate the injustice of a
discrimination, even on the most subtile
calculations of equity, abstracted from
the obligation of contract.

The difficulties too of regulating the
details of a plan for that purpose, which
would have even the semblance of
equity, would be found immense. It
may well be doubted whether they
would not be insurmountable, and re-
plete with such absurd, as well as in-
equitable consequences, as to disgust
even the proposers of the measure.

As a specimen of its capricious operation, it will be sufficient to notice the
effect it would have upon two persons,
who may be supposed two years ago to
have purchased, each, securities at three
shillings in the pound, and one of them
to retain those bought by him, till the
discrimination should take place; the
other to have parted with those bought
by him, within a month past, at nine
shillings. The former, who had had most
confidence in the government, would in
this case, only receive at the rate of three
shillings and the interest; while the latter,
who had had less confidence, would receive, *for what cost him the same money*,
at the rate of nine shillings, and his representative, *standing in his place*, would be
entitled to a like rate.

The impolicy of a discrimination results from two considerations; one, that
it proceeds upon a principle destructive
of that *quality* of the public debt, or the
stock of the nation, which is essential to
its capacity for answering the purposes
of money — that is, the *security of transfer;* the other, that as well on this account, as because it includes a breach of
faith, it renders property in the funds
less valuable; consequently induces lenders to demand a higher premium for what
they lend, and produces every other inconvenience of a bad state of public
credit.

It will be perceived at first sight, that
the transferable quality of stock, is essential to its operation as money; and that
this depends on the idea of complete
security to the transferee, and a firm per-
suasion, that no distinction can, in any
circumstances, be made between him
and the original proprietor.

The precedent of an invasion of this
fundamental principle, would of course
tend to deprive the community of an advantage, with which no temporary saving
could bear the least comparison.

And it will as readily be perceived,
that the same cause would operate a
diminution of the value of stock in the
hands of the first, as well as of every
other holder. The price which any man,
who should incline to purchase, would be
willing to give for it, would be in a compound ratio to the immediate profit it
afforded, and the chance of the continuance of his profit. If there was supposed
to be any hazard of the latter, the risk
would be taken into the calculation, and
either there would be no purchase at all,

or it would be at a proportionably less price.

For this diminution of the value of stock, every person, who should be about to lend to the government, would demand compensation; and would add to the actual difference between the nominal and the market value, an equivalent for the chance of greater decrease; which, in a precarious state of public credit, is always to be taken into the account.

Every compensation of this sort, it is evident, would be an absolute loss to the government.

In the preceding discussion of the impolicy of a discrimination, the injurious tendency of it to those who continue to be the holders of the securities they received from the government, has been explained. Nothing need be added on this head, except that this is an additional, and interesting light, in which the injustice of the measure may be seen. It would not only divest present proprietors, by purchase, of the rights they had acquired under the sanction of public faith; but it would depreciate the property of the remaining original holders.

It is equally unnecessary to add any thing to what has been already said, to demonstrate the fatal influence, which the principle of discrimination would have on the public credit.

But there is still a point in view in which it will appear, perhaps, even more exceptionable, than in either of the former: It would be repugnant to an express provision of the Constitution of the United States. This provision is, that "all debts contracted, and engagements entered into, before the adoption of that Constitution, shall be as valid against the United States under it, as under the confederation;" which amounts to a constitutional ratification of the contracts respecting the debt, in the state in which they existed under the confederation. And resorting to that standard, there can be no doubt, that the rights of assignees and original holders must be considered as equal.

In exploding thus fully the principle of discrimination, the Secretary is happy in reflecting, that he is only the advocate of what has been already sanctioned by the formal and express authority of the government of the Union, in these emphatic terms — "The remaining class of creditors, (say Congress, in their circular address to the states, of the 26th of April, 1783,) is composed, partly of such of our fellow-citizens as originally lent to the public the use of their funds, or have since manifested *most confidence* in their country, by receiving transfers from the lenders; and partly of those whose property has been either advanced or assumed for the public service. To *discriminate* the merits of these several descriptions of creditors, would be a task equally unnecessary and invidious. If the voice of humanity plead more loudly in favour of some than of others, the voice of policy, no less than of justice, pleads in favour of all. A WISE NATION will never permit those who relieve the wants of their country, or who *rely most* on its *faith,* its *firmness,* and its *resources,* when either of them is distrusted, to suffer by the event."

The Secretary, concluding that a discrimination between the different classes of creditors of the United States, cannot with propriety be made, proceeds to examine whether a difference ought to be permitted to *remain* between them and another description of public creditors — those of the states individually.

The Secretary, after mature reflection on this point, entertains a full conviction, that an assumption of the debts of the particular states by the union, and a like provision for them, as for those of the union, will be a measure of sound policy and substantial justice.

It would, in the opinion of the Secretary, contribute, in an eminent degree, to an orderly, stable, and satisfactory arrangement of the national finances.

Admitting, as ought to be the case, that a provision must be made in some way or other for the entire debt; it will follow, that no greater revenues will be required, whether that provision be made wholly by the United States, or partly by them, and partly by the states separately.

The principal question then must be, whether such a provision cannot be more conveniently and effectually made, by one general plan issuing from one authority, than by different plans originating in different authorities?

In the first case there can be no competition for resources; in the last, there must be such a competition. The consequences of this, without the greatest caution, on both sides, might be interfering regulations, and thence collision and confusion: Particular branches of industry might also be oppressed by it. The most productive objects of revenue are not numerous. Either these must be wholly engrossed by one side, which might lessen the efficacy of the provisions by the other; or both must have recourse to the same objects in different modes, which might occasion an accumulation upon them, beyond what they could properly bear. If this should not happen, the caution requisite to avoiding it, would prevent the revenue's deriving the full benefit of each object. The danger of interference and of excess would be apt to impose restraints very unfriendly

to the complete command of those resources, which are the most convenient; and to compel the having recourse to others, less eligible in themselves, and less agreeable to the community.

The difficulty of an effectual command of the public resources, in case of separate provisions for the debt, may be seen in another and perhaps more striking light. It would naturally happen that different states, from local considerations, would, in some instances, have recourse to different objects; in others, to the same objects, in different degrees, for procuring the funds of which they stood in need. It is easy to conceive how this diversity would affect the aggregate revenue of the country. By the supposition, articles which yielded a full supply in some states, would yield nothing, or an insufficient product in others; and hence the public revenue would not derive the full benefit of those articles, from state regulations: neither could the deficiencies be made good by those of the union. It is a provision of the national constitution, that "all duties, imposts, and excises, shall be uniform throughout the United States." And as the general government would be under a necessity, from motives of policy, of paying regard to the duty which may have been previously imposed upon any article, though but in a single state; it would be constrained, either to refrain wholly from any further imposition upon such article, where it had been already rated as high as was proper; or to confine itself to the difference between the existing rate, and what the article would reasonably bear. Thus the preoccupancy of an article by a single state, would tend to arrest or abridge the impositions of the union on that article. And as it is supposeable, that a great variety of articles might be placed in this situation, by dissimilar arrangements of the particular states, it is evident, that the aggregate revenue of the country would be likely to be very materially contracted by the plan of separate provisions.

If all the public creditors receive their dues from one source, distributed with an equal hand, their interest will be the same. And having the same interests, they will unite in the support of the fiscal arrangements of the government; as these, too, can be made with more convenience, where there is no competition: These circumstances combined, will ensure to the revenue laws a more ready and more satisfactory execution.

If, on the contrary, there are distinct provisions, there will be distinct interests, drawing different ways. That union and concert of views, among the creditors, which in every government is of great importance to their security, and to that of public credit, will not only not exist, but will be likely to give place to mutual jealousy and opposition: and from this cause, the operation of the systems which may be adopted, both by the particular states, and by the union, with relation to their respective debts, will be in danger of being counteracted.

There are several reasons which render it probable, that the situation of the state creditors would be worse than that of the creditors of the union, if there be not a national assumption of the state debts. Of these it will be sufficient to mention two; one, that a principal branch of revenue is exclusively vested in the union; the other, that a state must always be checked in the imposition of taxes on articles of consumption, from the want of power to extend the same regulation to the other states, and from the tendency of partial duties to injure its industry and commerce. Should the state creditors stand upon a less eligible footing than the others, it is unnatural to expect they would see with pleasure a provision for them. The influence which their dissatisfaction might have, could not but operate injuriously, both for the creditors and the credit of the United States.

Hence it is even the interest of the creditors of the union, that those of the individual states should be comprehended in a general provision: Any attempt to secure to the former, either exclusive or peculiar advantages, would materially hazard their interests.

Neither would it be just, that one class of the public creditors should be more favoured than the other. The objects for which both descriptions of the debt were contracted, are in the main the same. Indeed, a great part of the particular debts of the States has arisen from assumptions by them on account of the union. And it is most equitable, that there should be the same measure of retribution for all.

There is an objection, however, to an assumption of the state debts, which deserves particular notice.

It may be supposed, that it would increase the difficulty of an equitable settlement between them and the United States.

The principles of that settlement, whenever they shall be discussed, will require all the moderation and wisdom of the government. In the opinion of the Secretary, that discussion, till further lights are obtained, would be premature.

All, therefore, which he would now think advisable on the point in question, would be, that the amount of the debts assumed and provided for, should be charged to the respective states, to abide an eventual arrangement. This, the

United States, as assignees to the creditors, would have an indisputable right to do. . . .

Deeply impressed, as the Secretary is, with a full and deliberate conviction, that the establishment of public credit, upon the basis of a satisfactory provision for the public debt, is, under the present circumstances of this country, the true desideratum towards relief from individual and national embarrassments; that without it, these embarrassments will be likely to press still more severely upon the community — He cannot but indulge an anxious wish, that an effectual plan for that purpose may, during the present session, be the result of the united wisdom of the legislature.

He is fully convinced, that it is of the greatest importance, that no further delay should attend the making of the requisite provision; not only because it will give a better impression of the good faith of the country, and will bring earlier relief to the creditors; both which

circumstances are of great moment to public credit; but, because the advantages to the community from raising stock, as speedily as possible, to its natural value, will be incomparably greater than any that can result from its continuance below that standard. No profit, which could be derived from purchases in the market, on account of the government, to any practical extent, would be an equivalent for the loss which would be sustained by the purchases of foreigners at a low value. Not to repeat, that governmental purchases, to be honourable, ought to be preceded by a provision. Delay, by disseminating doubt, would sink the price of stock; and as the temptation to foreign speculations, from the lowness of the price, would be too great to be neglected, millions would probably be lost to the United States.

All of which is humbly submitted.
ALEXANDER HAMILTON,
Secretary of the Treasury

THE DEBATE IN THE UNITED STATES HOUSE OF REPRESENTATIVES

Important steps taken in the United States House of Representatives relative to the federal and state debts in the year 1790:

JANUARY 14	Hamilton's First Report on the Public Credit received by the House.
FEBRUARY 22	Madison's proposal to discriminate between original investors and current holders of the evidences of debt defeated 36 to 13. Main provisions for funding the federal domestic debt approved without a record vote.
APRIL 12	Proposal for the national government to assume the state debts temporarily defeated 31 to 29.
JULY 16	The residence act passed providing the national capitol should remain in Philadelphia ten years and then be established permanently on the banks of the Potomac.
JULY 24	Motion to disagree with the Senate's action in approving the assumption of state debts defeated 32 to 29.
JULY 26	Approval of assumption by the federal government of the state debts carried 34 to 28.

SPECULATION

JAMES JACKSON,[1] *Georgia.*

(January 28, 1790)

The report of the Secretary of the Treasury, Mr. Speaker, embraces subjects of the utmost magnitude, which ought not to be lightly taken up, or hastily concluded upon.[2] It appears to me to contain two important objects, worthy of our most serious and indefatigable disquisition. The first is, that all idea of discrimination among the public creditors, as original holders and transferees, ought to be done away; and on this head, I must own to you, sir, that I formerly coincided in something like the same opinion, but circumstances have occurred to make me almost a convert to the other.

Since this report has been read in this House, a spirit of havoc, speculation, and ruin, has arisen, and been cherished by

[1] The "leather-lunged" leader of the agrarian opposition to Hamilton's measures. Very few securities were owned by the citizens of the sparsely settled, frontier state of Georgia.

[2] The opponents of Hamilton's funding scheme sought to delay action by the House; the proponents urged prompt action.

The following excerpts are from *Annals of Congress,* 1st Cong., 2 vols., 1789–1791 (Gales and Seaton edition), I, 1094–1101; I, 1137–1159; I and II, 1163–1296; II, 1535–1700. *The outline of the steps taken and all footnotes have been added by the present editor.*

people who had an access to the information the report contained, that would
have made a Hastings blush to have been
connected with, though long inured to
preying on the vitals of his fellow men.
Three vessels, sir, have sailed within a
fortnight from this port, freighted for
speculation; they are intended to purchase up the State and other securities
in the hands of the uninformed, though
honest citizens of North Carolina, South
Carolina, and Georgia. My soul rises in-
dignant at the avaricious and immoral
turpitude which so vile a conduct
displays.

Then, sir, as to the other object of the
report — the assumption of the State
debts by the General Government — it
is a question of delicacy as well as importance. The States ought to be consulted on this point; some of them may
be against the measure; but surely it will
be prudent in us to delay deciding upon
a subject that may give umbrage to the
community.

THEODORE SEDGWICK,[3] *Massachusetts.*
   (January 28, 1790)
   I believe the House at present have not
come to a conclusion in their own opinion, on the various circumstances which
is necessary to be attended to in the report of the Secretary of the Treasury,
therefore, I think some delay is necessary; but it should be as early a day as
we could act upon it understandingly.
The ardent expectations of the people on
this subject want no other demonstration
than the numerous body of citizens
assembled within these walls. And while
the public expectation is kept thus alive,

[3] A leading lawyer of Western Massachusetts
closely allied to the Boston commercial interests
and an investor in government securities. Despite a humble origin, his manner is reported to
have been aristocratic and overbearing toward
common people.

and in suspense, gentlemen cannot but
suppose designs will be framed and
prosecuted that may be injurious to the
community. For, although I do not believe that speculation, to a certain degree, is baneful in its effects upon society,
yet, when it is extended too far, it becomes a real evil, and requires the Administration to divert or suppress it. If
the capital employed in merchandise is
taken from that branch of the public
interest, and employed in speculations no
way useful in increasing the labor of the
community, such speculation would be
pernicious. The employment of the time
of merchants in this way, in addition to
the employment of their capital, is a
serious and alarming circumstance. A
spirit of gambling is of such evil tendency, that every legislative endeavor
should be made to suppress it. From
these considerations, I take it, Mr.
Speaker, that there are two things very
evident — first, that the postponement
should be so long as to enable us to enter
upon the task with understanding; and
that this pernicious temper, or spirit of
speculation, should be counteracted at as
early a period as can possibly take place.

JAMES JACKSON, *Georgia.*
   (January 28, 1790)
   I know, sir, that there is, and will be,
speculations in the funds of every nation
possessed of public debt: but they are
not such as the present report has given
rise to, by the advantage those at the
seat of Government obtained of learning
the plan contemplated by the principal
of the Treasury Department, before
others had heard a word thereof. If we
had either received this report privately,
or not sat in a large city, then, sir, none
of these speculations would have arisen,
because Congress could have devised
means of diffusing the information so

generally as to prevent any of its ill effects. Under these impressions, I am led to express my ardent wish to God, that we had been on the banks of the Susquehanna or Potomac, or at any place in the woods, and out of the neighborhood of a populous city; all my unsuspecting fellow-citizens might then have been warned of their danger, and guarded themselves against the machinations of the speculators. To some gentlemen, characters of this kind may appear to be of utility; but I, sir, view them in a different light; they are as rapacious wolves seeking whom they may devour, and preying upon the misfortunes of their fellow men, taking an undue advantage of their necessities. This, sir, is the sentiment of my heart, and I will always use its language. I say, sir, whatever might be the happy effects of speculations in other countries, it has had the most unhappy and pernicious effects in this. Look at the gallant veteran, who nobly led your martial bands in the hour of extreme danger, whose patriotic soul acknowledged no other principle than that his life was the property of his country, and who evinced it by his repeated exposures to a vengeful enemy. See him deprived of those limbs which he sacrificed in your service! And behold his virtuous and tender wife sustaining him and his children in a wilderness, lonely, exposed to the arms of savages, where he and his family have been driven by this useful class of citizens, these speculators, who have drained from him the pittance which a grateful country had afforded him, in reward for his bravery and toils, and a long catalogue of merits. Nor is their insatiable avarice yet satisfied, while their remains a single class of citizens who retain the evidence of their demands upon the public; the State debts are to become an object for them

to prey upon, until other citizens are driven into scenes of equal distress. Is it not the duty of the House to check this spirit of devastation? It most assuredly is. If, by the ill-timed promulgation of this report, we have laid the foundation for the calamity, ought we not to counteract it? This may be done by postponing the subject, until the sense of the State Legislatures is obtained with respect to their particular debts. Then these men may send off other vessels to countermand their former orders; and, perhaps, we may yet save the distant inhabitants from being plundered by these harpies.

ELIAS BOUDINOT,[4] *New Jersey.*
(January 28, 1790)
. . . (I) should be sorry if, on this occasion, the House should decide that speculations in the funds are violations of either the moral or political law. A government hardly exists in which such speculation is disallowed; but it must, at the same time, be admitted, that every thing of this kind has proper bounds, which may be too small or too great. If you will not permit your creditor to transfer his debt, you deprive the Commonwealth of a great part of her credit and capital: on the other hand, if speculation is carried on to such a degree, as to divert the funds of productive labor into the pursuit of visionary objects, or destroys them, the community clearly loses the use of so much of its capital, which is a considerable evil. . . . (I agree) with gentlemen, that the spirit of speculation had now risen to an alarming height; but the only way to prevent its future effect, is to give the public funds a degree of stability as soon as possible.

[4] Formerly President of the Continental Congress, now leader of the New Jersey delegation. A cultured and wealthy gentleman and a heavy speculator in government securities.

FUNDING AT FACE VALUE

ELIAS BOUDINOT, *New Jersey.*

(February 8, 1790)

I conceive, Mr. Chairman, after duly considering the momentous circumstances I have brought to your attention, there is no man possessed of the principles of common honesty, within the sound of my voice, that will hesitate to conclude with me, that we are bound by every principle of honor, justice, and policy, to fund the debt of the United States, which has been one great means, under heaven, of securing to us our independence. I presume, sir, on this point we shall have no dispute. All that remains, then, for our consideration, is the manner and means of accomplishing it.

We must view it as a debt of honor, from the nature of the contract, from the objects effected, and the happy state we are now in. The principles of interest call loudly upon us to complete the business so happily begun. The Secretary, in the report before us, observes, with great justice, that exigencies are to be expected to occur in the affairs of nations, in which there will be a necessity for borrowing, and particularly in a country like this, possessed of little moneyed capital. How much, then, is it our interest to secure our public credit on a stable and sure foundation? Besides this, it is our interest in another point of view; by this means we shall introduce a medium into circulation which will give a spring to the agriculture, commerce, and manufactures of the Union.

Our policy also guides us into the adoption of some such measure as is proposed in the report. A punctual performance of our public engagements will invite moneyed men, in the days of distress, to lend us every pecuniary aid. Our debt undoubtedly is large; but not so large as might have been reasonably expected, considering the magnitude of the object we have successfully accomplished; but it can by no means be considered so large as to prevent us from an attempt to discharge it.

JAMES JACKSON, *Georgia.*

(February 9, 1790)

But why, Mr. Chairman, should we hasten on this business of funding? Are our debts ascertained? The report of the Secretary of the Treasury proposes that we should not only fund the debts that are ascertained, but the unliquidated and unsettled debts due from the Continent; nor does the plan stop here; it proposes that we should assume the payment of the State debts — debts to us totally unknown. Many of the States, sir, have not yet ascertained what they owe; and if we do not know the amount of what we owe, or are to be indebted, shall we establish funds? Shall we put our hands into the pockets of our constituents, and appropriate moneys for uses we are undetermined of? But more especially shall we do this, when, in doing it, it is indisputably certain, that the incumbrance will more than exceed all the benefits and conveniences? Gentlemen may come forward, perhaps, and tell me, that funding the public debt will increase the circulating medium of the country, by means of its transferable quality; but this is denied by the best informed men. The funding of the debt will occasion enormous taxes for the payment of the interest. These taxes will bear heavily, both on agriculture and commerce. It will be charging the active and industrious citizen, who pays his share of the taxes, to pay the indolent and idle creditor who receives them, to be spent and wasted in the course of the year, without any hope of a future reproduction; for the new capital which they acquire must have existed in the country before, and must have been employed, as all capitals are, in maintaining productive labor. Thus the honest and hard-working part of the community will promote the ease and luxury of men of wealth; such a system may benefit large cities, like Philadelphia and New York, but the remote parts of the continent will not feel the invigorating warmth of the American treasury; in the proportion that it benefits the one, it will depress another.

SAMUEL LIVERMORE,[1] *New Hampshire.*
    (February 9, 1790)

For my part, I consider the foreign and domestic debts to carry with them very material distinctions. The one is not like a debt, while the other has all the true qualities of one. However gentlemen may think on this subject, there is a great difference between the merits of that debt which was lent the United States in real coin, by disinterested persons, not concerned or benefited by the Revolution, and at a low rate of interest, and those debts which have been accumulating upon the United States, at the rate of six per cent interest, and which were not incurred for efficient money lent, but for depreciated paper, or services done at exorbitant rates, or for goods or provisions supplied at more than their real worth, by those who received all the benefits arising from our change of condition. It is within the knowledge of every gentleman, that a very considerable part of our domestic loan-office debt arose in this manner. It is well known

---

[1] At this time, both Chief Justice of the Superior Court of New Hampshire and a member of the United States House of Representatives. He had a reputation for outspoken honesty.

that loan-office certificates were issued as a kind of circulating medium, when the United States were in such straits for cash that they could not raise the necessary supplies in any other way. And it is very well known, that those who sold goods or provisions for this circulating medium, raised their prices from six to ten shillings at least.

There is another observation I would beg leave to make. The prices at which our supplies were procured were such, even in hard money, that it might be said specie had depreciated, or, what amounted to the same thing, the commodities were sold for more than their current price; in many cases, half the price would now purchase the same thing. If so, there is as much reason that we should now consider these public securities in a depreciated state, as every holder of them has considered them from that time to this. There was a period at which they were considered of no greater value than three or four shillings in the pound; at this day they are not at more than eight or ten. If this, then, is the case, why should Congress put it upon the same footing as the foreign debt, for which they received a hard dollar for every dollar they engaged to pay? Could any possible wrong be done to those who hold the domestic debt by estimating it at its current value? I do not speak of those only who have speculated in certificates. With respect to them, I do not see how a difference can be made. By the resolutions of Congress, and from the face of the papers, it appears that they were transferable.

It may be said, that there was some part of the domestic debt incurred by loans of hard money. There might be a small part lent in this way, but it was very small indeed, compared with the whole of the domestic debt. It is in the memory of every gentleman, that, before the beginning of the Revolution, every State issued paper money; it answered the exigencies of Government in a considerable degree. The United States issued a currency of the same nature, which answered their purposes, except in some particular cases, and these were effected by loans of certain sums of hard money. If any distinctions are to be made among the domestic creditors, it ought to be made in favor of such only, and that in consequence of the origin of the debt; while the great mass given for the depreciated paper, or provisions sold at double prices, ought to be liquidated at its real value. I cannot think it injustice to reduce the interest on those debts. I should therefore be against passing this resolution, if it carries in it the idea of paying the principal and interest, according to the face of the paper. It is well known, that a large proportion of this domestic debt was incurred for paper money lent. To be sure Congress acknowledged its value equal to its name; but this was done on a principle of policy, in order to prevent the rapid depreciation which was taking place. But money lent in this depreciated and depreciating state can hardly be said to be lent from a spirit of patriotism; it was a mere speculation in public securities. They hoped, by putting their money in the loan-office, though in a depreciated state, to receive hard money for it by and by. I flatter myself this prediction will never be effected.

The Secretary of the Treasury has offered some alternatives to the creditors, out of which they may make their election; but it seems to me that they, all of them, propose a reduction in the principal and interest, that they may have an annuity of two-thirds at six per centum, or for the whole sum at four per centum,

or they may accept of the other terms. Though this may make a reduction favorable to the public, yet this is not such a reduction as justice, in my opinion, requires; and as the resolution before the committee is intended to make way for the adoption of those principles, I shall vote against it, though I would rather it was passed over for the present, in order to see what is the sense of the House in making a specific provision for the payment of the debt.

ELIAS BOUDINOT, *New Jersey.*
(February 9, 1790)

. . . Instead of being judges, or arbitrators, on this occasion, we are parties to the contract; nor is our case varied by the dissolution of the old Confederacy, because the existing Constitution has expressly recognized the engagements made under the former. All debts contracted before the adoption of this Constitution shall be as valid against the United States, under this Government, as under the Confederation. Now is the moment to establish the principle; if the Constitution admits the borrowing of money, or paying for supplies, to be a contract, we are one of the parties to this contract, and all idea of being arbiters must vanish. We cannot judge in our own cause.

The case will now stand clear: We owe a debt contracted for a valuable consideration. The evidences of our debt are in the hands of our creditors, and we are called upon to discharge them; if we have it in our power, we ought to consider ourselves bound to do it, on every principle of honor, of justice, and of policy. But as we have not the ability to pay the whole off, nor, perhaps, the whole interest, we must endeavor to make such a modification as will enable us to satisfy every one. Not that this modification shall take place without the consent of the creditors; this would be improper and unjust. Each part is as much to be consulted on this occasion, as it was at the time of the first contract. If, then, Congress is bound by the first contract, no gentleman can say we are judges. If we are parties, what would be the decision before a court of justice? The creditor produces my bond, by which I have bound myself to pay a hundred dollars; I cannot gainsay the fact; no man is allowed to plead that he has made a bad bargain, and that, at other times, he could have purchased what he got of the creditor at half the sum he was forced to allow him. The inquiry with the judges is not whether the debtor made a good bargain or not, but whether he did it fairly and voluntarily. We are in the same predicament if we fairly and honestly received the *quid pro quo;* we are bound, as parties to the honest performance of the contract, to discharge the debt; otherwise, what avails the clause in the Constitution, declaring all debts contracted, and engagements entered into, before its adoption, to be as valid against the present Government as they were under the old Confederation? The debt was *bona fide* contracted; it was acknowledged by the United States; and the creditor received a certificate as the evidence of his debt. It is immaterial to us what he did with it. I confess, if the original holder was to come forward, and say that he had been robbed of such evidence, we ought not to pay it until the point was ascertained in a court of justice.

. . . I confess we are not warranted to charge our constituents with unreasonable burdens; and therefore, I presume we are authorized to make propositions to our creditors for a more convenient mode of payment than what was originally contracted for; but this is optional with them. If they refuse to listen to us, and insist upon their just claim, we must satisfy it as far as we have the ability; thus far, I presume, we may fairly go, in regard to the domestic debt.

FISHER AMES,[2] *Massachusetts.*

(February 9, 1790)

. . . What, let me inquire, will be the pernicious consequences resulting from the establishment of this doctrine [*i.e.* scaling down of the debt]? Will it not be subversive of every principle on which public contracts are founded? The evidences of the debt, possessed by the creditors of the United States, cannot, in reason, justice, or policy, be considered in any other light than as public bonds, for the redemption and payment of which the property and labor of the whole people are pledged. The only just idea is, that when the public contract a debt with an individual, that it becomes personified, and that with respect to this contract, the powers of Government shall never legislate. If this was not the case, it would destroy the effect it was intended to produce; no individual would be found willing to trust the Government, if he supposed the Government had the inclination and power, by virtue of a mere major vote, to set aside the terms of the engagement. If the public in such a case is, as I have said, personified, what conceivable difference is there,

[2] A scholarly and eloquent speaker, he was a leading New England Federalist. John Quincy Adams wrote in 1809: "Mr. Ames was a man of genius and of virtue — he meant well to his country, and served her with fidelity according to his best judgment. But at a very early period of his public life, he connected himself with Hamilton, his bank and his funding system, in a manner which warped his judgment and trammelled the freedom of his mind for the remainder of his days." (*American Principles: A Review of Works of Fisher Ames,* Boston, 1809, No. 1.)

except in favor of the creditor, between the public and an individual in the case? If, then, the public contract is a solemn obligation upon us, we are bound to its true and faithful performance. What is the object for which men enter into society, but to secure their lives and property? What is the usual means of acquiring property between man and man? The best right to property is acquired by the consent of the last owner. If, then, an individual is possessed of property, in consequence of this right, how can Government, founded on this social compact, pretend to exercise the right of divesting a man of that object, which induced him to combine himself with the society? Every gentleman may determine this question by his own feelings. Shall it be said that this Government, evidently established for the purpose of securing property, that, in its first act, it divested its citizens of seventy millions of money, which is justly due to the individuals who have contracted with Government! I believe those gentlemen, who are apprehensive for the liberties and safety of their fellow-citizens, under the efficiency of the present Constitution, will find real cause of alarm from the establishment of the present doctrine. I have heard, that in the East Indies, the stock of the labor and property of the Empire is the property of the Prince; that it is held at his will and pleasure; but this is a slavish doctrine, which I hope we are not prepared to adopt here. But I will not go further into a consideration of the idea of discrimination. I will ask, though, is this country ever to be in a settled and quiet state? Must every transaction that took place, during the course of the last war, be ripped up? Shall we never have done with the settlement and liquidation of our accounts? If this is the case, what kind of rights will the people have in

their property? None but the will of the Government. And will this tend to the establishment of public credit? What security will they derive from a new promise? None. They will know that this can be set aside equally with the other, provided it is deemed expedient. What mischief will follow this idea? The public faith destroyed, our future credit will be a mere vapor; and all this risk is to be run for the sake of — what? Of saving something to the public? No; the public will lose by the transaction more than they will gain; our justice will be impeached, and foreigners will feel themselves happy, that they have it in their power, by violence, to procure to themselves that which we deny to our own citizens. Such a mere arbitrary act of power can never be exercised on the part of Government, but to the destruction of the essential rights of the people, and will finally terminate in a dissolution of the social compact.

SAMUEL LIVERMORE, *New Hampshire.*
(February 9, 1790)
. . . That the late Congress had, at all times, from their first institution, the power to contract debts, for the benefit of the United States, cannot be denied; and that we are authorized to pay such debts, is equally certain. But this by no means contravenes the opinion of those gentlemen who think that the whole may be properly considered and discharged at the rate which justice requires; for the same argument which is urged for the payment of the public securities at their nominal value, might be urged in favor of paying off the Continental debts of credit [Revolutionary paper money], according to the sums expressed on the face of them.[3] They were issued with as much

3 Hamilton's funding plan did not contemplate the redemption at face value of the paper money

confidence, and were received with as firm a reliance on the public faith, as any species of securities whatever; yet, it seems to be given up on all hands, that the owners of the old Continental paper bills ought not to be paid according to their nominal value. Perhaps it may be said, on comparing them with the loan-office certificates, that the United States had not the benefit of that money; but had they not the value of it? It will be answered, that when the money was first issued, Congress had nearly the value for it; but afterwards the money greatly depreciated, and they had not the full value for it, yet the obligation to pay it is as explicit as words can make it. No advocate will be found for making all that money good. It has been thought proper, and it is just, that it should be reduced from its nominal value; if it is reduced on a scale of one hundred for one, the holders of it, I dare say, would cheerfully receive that sum. If the United States then had value for it, and they had not value for the certificates, who can doubt of the justice of reliquidating, and duly ascertaining the public debt? All I contend for is this, that the present Government pay the debts of the United States; but as the domestic part of the debt has been contracted in depreciated notes, that less interest should be paid upon it than six per cent. Six per cent was the usual interest upon the certificates when they were issued by Congress; but if the possessor has received no part of his six per cent until this time, that now the principal and interest be consolidated into one sum, hereafter to bear an interest of three or four per cent; then those citizens, who now stand as creditors of the Union, will find that part of their

issued by the Continental Congress. The funding act as finally passed provided for such redemption at one cent on the dollar.

property has been the most productive of any, much more productive than the property of the citizens of the United States has generally been. Those who lent their money to individuals before and during the late war, generally lost or suffered by the depreciation some three-quarters of the capital; nay, some thirty-nine fortieths. But is this the case of the domestic creditor of the United States? No! he will preserve his property, through the chaos of the Revolution, and be put now in a more eligible situation than he was at the time he loaned his money. The capital sum which he lent is now increased, and very rapidly increased, for six per cent is a very large interest. He will now receive 160 dollars for his 100, and putting that into the funds, at three or four per cent, he will find it more productive than any other method in which he could employ his money; for, I contend, that neither improved, nor unimproved lands, will give an interest near half of what the public creditor will receive. People who have held real property have sunk, with the taxes, and other losses, the greatest part of it, but the public creditor has let his run through the confusion of the Revolution, and nevertheless gets it returned to him safe; and, so far from being impaired, that it has prodigiously accumulated, not only in a manner superior to the property of his fellow-citizens, but superior to the foreigner who lent his money at four per cent. Justice and equity require, on the behalf of the community, that these people be content with reasonable profit. They ought not, therefore, to receive, on a funded debt, so much as six per cent; whether three or four, or something between three and four, would be a proper sum, I shall not pretend to determine. But I consider it a proper question for this committee to consider, in justice to those who are to pay, as well as to those who are to receive; nor do I believe the domestic creditors would be dissatisfied with it, provided they were sure of receiving this annual interest; for their debts, on such a footing, would be better to them than if they were established on an extravagant plan, that could never be effected, but which would be likely to throw the nation into confusion. Every body has suffered more or less by the depreciation, but the public creditors very little, in regard to that part of their property which they had deposited in the hands of Government: It is true, that it has slept; but it is now waked up to some purpose.

THOMAS SCOTT,[4] *Pennsylvania.*

(February 9, 1790)

. . . Is there any power of Government more frequently exercised than that of

[4] A political leader of Western Pennsylvania who represented commercial rather than agrarian interests. He opposed some of Hamilton's measures and supported others.

interfering with and modifying private contracts? In London, houses have been razed to their foundations; men's lands have been taken from them, and yet it was never thought that the Government ever acted wrong in the exercise of authority; private property must not only be subject to a change of shape, but sometimes to an absolute extinguishment, rather than a nation should sink, or the public safety be endangered. This power has been exercised at home; paper money, at one time, passed current, and was of value nearly equal to gold and silver; but the value expressed on the face of it was that of specie itself. What did the Government do when the depreciation had extended itself to a great degree? They laid violent hands upon it and it was scaled. Was that a violation of the public faith? If so, was it not necessary and inevitable? Why, then, is this the only contract that cannot be violated without a breach of public faith, or the loss of public credit?

DISCRIMINATION

JAMES JACKSON, *Georgia.*

(February 9, 1790)

The honorable gentlemen who are in opposition, contend, that no sort of discrimination ought to take place; yet from what they have let fall, on this occasion, I am led to believe that they favor that part of the report of the Secretary which makes a discrimination, in fact, equal to a loss of one-third of the principal. What will hold good in one case ought to hold good in another, and a discrimination might take place upon the same principles, between those to whom the Govern-

ment was originally indebted, and who have never received satisfaction therefor, and those who had nothing to do with the Government in the first transaction; but have merely speculated, and purchased up the evidence of an original debt. Some gentlemen think, that the claims of this latter class merit a greater degree of attention, because, by their actions, they seem to have evinced a greater degree of confidence in the Government than those who sold them. But, sir, these men have had more information, they have been at the seat of Government, and knew what was in contemplation before citizens of other parts of the Union could be acquainted with it. There has been no kind of proportion of knowledge between the two classes — to use the expression of a British Minister, the reciprocity has been all on one side. The people in this city are informed of all the motions of Government; they have sent out their money, in swift sailing vessels, to purchase up the property of uninformed citizens in the remote parts of the Union. Were those citizens acquainted with our present deliberations, and assured of the intention of Congress to provide for their just demands, they would be on an equal footing; they would not incline to throw away their property for considerations totally inadequate. Such attempts at fraud would justify the Government in interfering in the transactions between individuals, without a breach of the public faith. . . .

THOMAS SCOTT, *Pennsylvania.*

(February 10, 1790)

The gentleman from Massachusetts (Mr. Sedgwick), who has spoken since I was last up, has said something . . . which is well worthy of due consideration. He has told us that the most alarming consequences are to be apprehended from delaying this important business beyond the present session; that it will destroy the peace of the society, and endanger the Union itself. If that be the case, a skin for a skin, all that a man has he will give to save his life. If we are to be torn to pieces, or if the speculators will cut our throats, if we do not pay them twenty shillings for their half crown, I will consent to what you please; but, before I do this, I should like to know how this is to come about, and how we are to be distressed by the necessary delay of the business.

THEODORE SEDGWICK, *Massachusetts.*

(February 10, 1790)

I will express my idea on the point which the gentleman has made an inquiry respecting, in a few words. I said, that I conceived a delay of this business would endanger the peace of the Union by diminishing the energy of the Government, without which this Constitution would be of no value. These are considerations which must appear weighty and important. . . . A great and respectable body of our citizens are creditors of the United States. There are a variety of opinions prevailing respecting their claims, with respect to funding, discrimination, and interest. This diversity of opinion may probably irritate, and produce heats and animosities, which may terminate in forming factions among the people. The State debts may produce a difference between the General and particular Governments. If the matter is taken up as the business of a party, one may be pitted against the other, until, in the end, they disturb the public tranquillity, or sacrifice the general welfare to opposition and party spirit. Besides this, the reputation, the credit of the Government is at stake; the public expectation is alive to all the measures of Government at the present moment. They expect that justice and equity will be administered as far as the abilities of our country extend; it lies with the Legislature to realize this expectation. If Congress pursue the present inquiry, and come to a determination without delay, the public sentiment will be brought to a point, and a general acquiescence may be expected; but if it is postponed to a future session, such may be the effect of faction and disappointment during the recess, that the probability is, that no one party will comprise a sufficient number to comprehend the majority of the whole.

JAMES JACKSON, *Georgia.*

(February 10, 1790)

Do not gentlemen think there is some danger on the other side? Will there not be grounds of uneasiness when the soldier and meritorious citizen are called upon to pay the speculator more than ten times the amount they ever received from him for their securities? I believe, Mr. Chairman, there is more just reason of alarm on this than on the other side of the question.

JAMES MADISON,[1] *Virginia.*

(February 11, 1790)

It has been said, by some gentlemen, that the debt itself does not exist in the extent and form which is generally supposed. I confess, sir, I differ altogether from the gentlemen who take that ground. Let us consider, first, by whom the debt was contracted, and then let us consider to whom it is due. The debt was contracted by the United States, who, with respect to that particular transaction, were in a national capacity. The Government was nothing more than the agent or organ, by which the whole body of the people acted. The change in the Government which has taken place has enlarged its national capacity, but it has not varied the national obligation, with respect to the engagements entered into by that transaction. For, in like manner, the present Government is nothing more than the organ, or agent, of the public. The obligation which they are under, is precisely the same with that under which the debt was contracted; although the

Government has been changed, the nation remains the same. There is no change in our political duty, nor in the moral or political obligation. The language I now use, sir, is the language of the Constitution itself; it declares that all debts shall have the same validity against the United States, under the new, as under the old form of Government. The obligation remains the same, though I hope experience will prove that the ability has been favorably varied.

The next question is, to what amount the public are at present indebted? I conceive the question may be answered in a few words. The United States owe the value they received, which they acknowledge, and which they have promised to pay: what is that value? It is a certain sum in principal, bearing an interest of six per cent. No logic, no magic, in my opinion, can diminish the force of the obligation.

The only point on which we can deliberate is, to whom the payment is really due; for this purpose, it will be proper to take notice of the several descriptions of people who are creditors of the Union, and lay down some principles respecting them, which may lead us to a just and equitable decision. As there is a small part of the debt yet unliquidated, it may be well to pass it by and come to the great mass of the liquidated debt. It may here be proper to notice four classes into which it may be divided:

First. Original creditors, who have never alienated their securities.

Second. Original creditors who have alienated.

Third. Present holders of alienated securities.

Fourth. Intermediate holders, through whose hands securities have circulated.

---

[1] Madison had not previously participated in the debate. His speech made a profound impression. It revealed the fundamental cleavage between Hamilton and Madison, the differences in philosophy and class interest which were rapidly leading to the formation of two parties, the Federalists and the Anti-Federalists.

The only principles that can govern the decision on their respective pretensions, I take to be: 1. Public Justice; 2. Public Faith; 3. Public Credit; 4. Public Opinion.

With respect to the first class, there can be no difficulty. Justice is in their favor, for they have advanced the value which they claim; public faith is in their favor, for the written promise is in their hands; respect for public credit is in their favor, for if claims so sacred are violated, all confidence must be at an end; public opinion is in their favor, for every honest citizen cannot but be their advocate.

With respect to the last class, the intermediate holders, their pretensions, if they have any, will lead us into a labyrinth, for which it is impossible to find a clew. This will be the less complained of, because this class were perfectly free, both in becoming and ceasing to be creditors; and because, in general, they must have gained by their speculations.

The only rival pretensions then are those of the original creditors, who have assigned, and of the present holders of the assignments.

The former may appeal to justice, because the value of the money, the service, or the property advanced by them, has never been really paid to them.

They may appeal to good faith, because the value stipulated and expected, is not satisfied by the steps taken by the Government. The certificates put into the hands of the creditors, on closing their settlements with the public, were of less real value than was acknowledged to be due; they may be considered as having been forced, in fact, on the receivers. They cannot, therefore, be fairly adjudged an extinguishment of the debt. They may appeal to the motives for establishing public credit, for which justice and faith form the natural foundation. They may appeal to the precedent furnished by the compensation allowed to the army during the late war, for the depreciation of bills, which nominally discharged the debts. They may appeal to humanity, for the sufferings of the military part of the creditors can never be forgotten, while sympathy is an American virtue. To say nothing of the singular hardship, in so many mouths, of requiring those who have lost four-fifths or seven-eighths of their due, to contribute the remainder in favor of those who have gained in the contrary proportion.

On the other hand, the holders by assignment, have claims, which I by no means wish to depreciate. They will say, that whatever pretensions others may have against the public, these cannot effect the validity of theirs. That if they gain by the risk taken upon themselves, it is but the just reward of that risk. That as they hold the public promise, they have an undeniable demand on the public faith. That the best foundation of public credit is that adherence to literal engagements on which it has been erected by the most flourishing nations. That if the new Government should swerve from so essential a principle, it will be regarded by all the world as inheriting the infirmities of the old. Such being the interfering claims on the public, one of three things must be done; either pay both, reject wholly one or the other, or make a *composition* between them on some principle of equity. To pay both is perhaps beyond the public ability; and as it would far exceed the value received by the public, it will not be expected by the world, nor even by the creditors themselves. To reject wholly the claims of either is equally inadmissible; such a sacrifice of those who possess the written engagements would be fatal to the proposed establishment of public credit; it would moreover punish those who had put their trust in the public promises and resources. To make the other class the sole victims is an idea at which human nature recoils.

A composition, then, is the only expedient that remains; let it be a liberal one in favor of the present holders, let them have the highest price which has prevailed in the market; and let the residue belong to the original sufferers. This will not do perfect justice; but it will do more real justice, and perform more of the public faith, than any other expedient proposed. The present holders, where they have purchased at the lowest price of the securities, will have a profit that cannot reasonably be complained of; where they have purchased at a higher price, the profit will be considerable; and even the few who have purchased at the highest price cannot well be losers, with a well funded interest of six per cent. The original sufferers will not be fully indemnified; but they will receive, from their country, a tribute due to their merits, which, if it does not entirely heal their wounds, will assuage the pain of them. I am aware, that many plausible objections will lie against what I have suggested, some of which I foresee and will take some notice of. It will be said, that the plan is impracticable; should this be demonstrated, I am ready to renounce it; but it does not appear to me in that light. I acknowledge that such a scale as has often been a subject of conversation, is impracticable.

The discrimination proposed by me, requires nothing more than a knowledge of the present holders, which will be shown by the certificates; and of the original holders, which the office documents will show. It may be objected, that if the Government is to go beyond the literal into the equitable claims against the United States, it ought to go back to every case where injustice has been done. To this the answer is obvious: the case in question is not only different from others in point of magnitude and of practicability, but forces itself on the attention of the committee, as necessarily involved in the business before them. It may be objected, that public credit will suffer, especially abroad; I think this danger will be effectually obviated by the honesty and disinterestedness of the Government displayed in the measure, by a continuance of the punctual discharge of foreign interest, by the full provision to be made for the whole foreign debt, and the equal punctuality I hope to see in the future payments on the domestic debts. I trust also, that all future loans will be founded on a previous establishment of adequate funds; and that a situation, like the present, will be thereby rendered impossible.

I cannot but regard the present case as so extraordinary, in many respects, that the ordinary maxims are not strictly applicable to it. The fluctuations of stock in Europe, so often referred to, have no comparison with those in the United States. The former never exceeded 50, 60, or 70 per cent: can it be said, that because a Government thought this evil insufficient to justify an interference, it would view in the same light a fluctuation amounting to seven or eight hundred per cent?

I am of opinion, that were Great Britain, Holland, or any other country, to fund its debts precisely in the same situation as the American debt, some equitable interference of the Government would take place. The South Sea scheme, in which a change, amounting to one thousand per cent happened in the value of stock, is well known to have produced an interference, and without any injury whatever to the subsequent credit of the nation. It is true, that in many respects, the case differed from that of the United States; but, in other respects, there is a degree of similitude, which warrants the conjecture. It may be objected, that such a provision as I propose will exceed the public ability; I do not think the public unable to discharge honorably all its engagements, or that it will be unwilling, if the appropriations shall be satisfactory. I regret, as much as any member, the unavoidable weight and duration of the burdens to be imposed; having never been a proselyte to the doctrine, that public debts are public benefits. I consider them, on the contrary, as evils which ought to be removed as fast as honor and justice will permit, and shall heartily join in the means necessary for that purpose. I conclude with declaring, as my opinion, that if any case were to happen among individuals, bearing an analogy to that of the public, a Court of Equity would interpose for its redress; or that if a tribunal existed on earth, by which nations could be compelled to do right, the United States would be compelled to do something not dissimilar in its principles to what I have contended for.

ELIAS BOUDINOT, *New Jersey.*

(February 11, 1790)

. . . Influenced by a desire to do justice to every person connected with the public, I wished for the means of compensating the original holders, who had sold their certificates at a great loss; but I found the thing, upon long and careful examination, to be both unjust and impracticable.

The honorable gentleman tells us, that the debt was contracted for meritorious services, and inquires whether the credi-

tor received an adequate compensation in full discharge? I say, sir, this debt is still due, and that the person to whom it is due, has received nothing but a certificate as evidence of his claim; but then, if any of our first creditors have put another person in their shoes, the question will arise, are we to disown the act of the party himself? Are we to say, we will not be bound by your transfer, we will not treat with your representative, but insist upon a resettlement with you alone? But the same reasoning will oblige us to go further, and investigate all the claims of those who have received of the Government Continental money, which they afterwards parted with for ten, forty, or one hundred for one.

But, putting all this out of the question, and supposing the motion to be founded on principles of justice, I would ask how it is to be carried into execution? The nature of the public debt will demonstrate its impracticability. A great part of this debt was contracted by the clerks in office, who, when the Continental money was stopped, were supplied with some millions of dollars in loan-office certificates; they were given out in their names, and afterwards distributed among the farmers, mechanics, and others, who had furnished supplies, or performed services. Now, how is it possible that you can ever trace a certificate, under these circumstances, up to the man who was the original *bona fide* creditor? Not from the name on the face of the paper, because it is the name of the clerk in office, the mere agent of the public. Other certificates were taken out of the loan-office, by persons who were not concerned in making the loan; many neighbors sent money by one hand, who went and took out certificates in his own name, which he afterwards returned to the real lender. I have been entrusted myself with numerous commissions of this kind, when I have been going to the capital, where the loan-office was kept. Now, suppose, as has been the case, that I took $10,000 from ten of my neighbors, each $1000, and that I placed the whole in the Continental loan-office at Philadelphia, taking out therefore ten loan-office certificates of $1000 each, which, on my return, I gave to those who had sent their money by me; all these certificates had my name in them, and here I should appear to be the original holder of $10,000 without any right whatever, and the men who deserve much of their country, for the aid they furnished her in the hour of distress, are stripped in a moment of the greatest part of their property. I believe, if we adopt this motion, we shall give room for such scenes of enormity as humanity will be shocked at the bare prospect of. I am, therefore, clearly of opinion, that if the principle be ever so just, we ought to reject it on account of its impracticability.

WILLIAM LOUGHTON SMITH,[2] S. *Carolina.*
   (February 15, 1790)
   . . . For his part, having bestowed on it the most attentive consideration, he could assert, that the more he contemplated it [Madison's proposal for discrimination], the more he was impressed with a conviction that the proposition was unjust, impolitic, and impracticable. It consisted of two parts: The one was to take away the property of one person; the other was to give that property to another; and this by a voluntary interposition of the House, by a mere act of power, without the assent of the former, or without even the application of the latter. For it was remarkable, that the

original holders, who had alienated their certificates, had not come forward with this demand; and it is presumable, that, had they applied for redress, they would reject any indemnification which was the result of such manifest injustice. To prove that this was taking away the property of a citizen by force, he observed, that the purchaser had, by a fair purchase, acquired a right to the full amount of the sum expressed in the certificate, which it was not within the power of the House to divest him of. No tribunal on earth could lawfully deprive a man of his property fairly obtained. The purchaser bought under the act of Congress, making the securities transferable; and having given the market price, without fraud or imposition, he was, by virtue of such purchase, vested with the complete and absolute ownership of the certificate, as fully as the original holder; and had as much right to demand full payment as the original holder would have had, had the security been still in his hands. Even should the House refuse, by an act of power, to pay him more than half his demand, the other half would still remain against the public; it could not be extinguished. The debt would continually haunt them; the creditors would loudly clamor for justice, and sooner or later the balance would be paid. Then would they incur all the odium of a violation of private rights, without deriving to the public any advantage whatever. He considered the measure as doing a certain evil, that a possible good might result from it. This was not, in his opinion, the proper mode of doing good. Justice cannot be founded on injustice; and to take money out of the pocket of one man, to put it into that of another, is a precedent which may justify future interferences. This step would lead the House to others: for, if the principle be

_____
[2] Closely identified with the Charleston commercial elite and reportedly a heavy speculator in public funds.

a just one, then the Government should look into all the transactions and speculations of individuals, in order to correct them, and make retribution to every individual according to his losses. He was persuaded, that the true policy of a Legislative body was, to pursue the broad road of justice, clearly marked out before them; for it was an undeniable truth, that whenever they deviated into by-roads and trackless paths, without any other guide than their own imagination, they would get bewildered in a labyrinth of difficulties, and rejoice to trace back their steps, and regain the plain road. Now, the plain line of conduct is, to do strict justice, such as is enforced in judicial tribunals, between man and man, in a similar case. The debtor is bound to pay the debt to the holder of the security; the contract, between the giver of the bond and the person to whom it was given, is done away the moment the latter assigns it to another person.

JAMES JACKSON, *Georgia.*
(February 16, 1790)
The House were told much of the moral obligations we were under of paying our debts, and the impolicy and injustice of interfering with private contracts. The obligation, he believed, was no where denied; the debt was of the highest nature; it was the price of our independence: the only difficulty is, how that debt shall be discharged. He would here observe, that the justice of the plan before the House had not been so fully objected to, as the impracticability, although it had been asserted to be unjust by some of the gentlemen who had spoken.

*   *   *

But a gentleman (Mr. Lawrence) had told us, that equity has fixed rules, and that none of those rules would apply.

He agreed with them, that it was as necessary for a Court of Equity to be confined by rules as a Court of Law; but exclusive of the former case, he had mentioned there were two others, under which the present case came — misfortune and oversight. He would quote the authority of *Blackstone,* did he not expect he should, as in former instances, be complained of by that gentleman for it. Here, he said, had been one of the greatest misfortunes; a calamity attending a whole community, a Government unable to pay its debts. Here was likewise an oversight equal to it. Was it possible for the poor soldier, uninformed, to foresee, when he sold his certificates, that they would rise to the present value? Or that he could anticipate the present day, and a second revolution? Equity, then, requires some mode of justice, and the tribunal exists somewhere. I believe, with my friend from Pennsylvania (Mr. Scott), that we are the tribunal; for equity must exist somewhere, or the Government is at end. The Courts of Law, and common Courts of Equity, have no power to interfere; they cannot compel us to their mode of funding our debts. The injury cries aloud for redress; iniquity is in the land, and we are bound, by every principle of justice, to step forward, and do what justice we can.

But perfect justice cannot be done, say gentlemen, and therefore we should not attempt the business at all. The consequences of this doctrine are fatal; they tend to a deprivation of all Courts of Justice: for there is no instance which can be adduced, where, what is termed justice, is reconciled to the opinions of all, and where some objection cannot be raised.

*   *   *

This public opinion is in favor of the original creditor; it is impossible to be otherwise. The people of America are a grateful people; and they cannot, with indifference, view the earnings of those who established their independence, converted into the coffers of the wealthy and ambitious. The speculator, he contended, was already more than satisfied, if it was only on the principle of interest which had accrued for six, seven, and eight years past, and which they had speculated on since.

He then observed, that, conceiving those objections raised by the opposition refuted, the next consideration was the impracticability.

*　*　*

A gentleman had declared it impracticable; because the quartermasters of the late army, and the clerks of office, received the certificates in their own names; and, as an instance, quotes himself as having received large sums in that manner. But, said he, are not the books and documents remaining? Is there not evidence still existing of the original creditor? That gentleman's own objection proves it. We will call him as an evidence; and there is no doubt but mankind are not so debased, but that many other similar confessions will come forward. Besides, there could be a touchstone applied equal to what the highest Court of Equity used, and there is little fear but the truth would be found out, and a detection made of fraudulent claims. The impracticability, he observed, was out of the question, with respect to the speculator, who would receive the highest market price.

But the public accounts were many of them lost. Make it worth the time of the original creditor, and this would be in a great measure obviated.

Again, says a gentleman (Mr. Sedgwick), the certificates are in fictitious names, and he knows an instance in Boston. Then that gentleman is likewise good evidence; and the claim, from his testimony, would be invalidated; but if not, the same equitable proof would be required.

. . . . If, however, the claimant did not come forward, he would contend that the public, not the speculator, ought to be the gainer; that the public here, would possess the same right as an estate left without an heir.

JAMES MADISON, *Virginia.*
  (February 18, 1790)
It could not have escaped the committee, that the gentlemen to whom he was opposed, had reasoned on this momentous question as on an ordinary case in a Court of Law; that they had equally strained all the maxims that could favor the purchasing, or be adverse to the original holder; and that they had dwelt with equal pleasure on every circumstance which could brighten the pretensions of the former, or discredit those of the latter. He had not himself attempted, nor did he mean to undervalue the pretensions of the actual holders. In stating them, he had even used as strong terms as they themselves could have dictated; but beyond a certain point he could not go. He must renounce every sentiment which he had hitherto cherished, before his complaisance could admit that America ought to erect the monuments of her gratitude, not to those who saved her liberties, but to those who had enriched themselves in her funds.

All that he wished was, that the claims of the original holders, not less than those of the actual holders, should be fairly examined and justly decided. They had been invalidated by nothing yet urged. A debt was fairly contracted; according to justice and good faith, it ought to have been paid in gold or silver; a piece of paper only was substituted. Was this paper equal in value to gold or silver? No. It was worth, in the market, which the argument for the purchasing holders makes the criterion, no more than one-eighth or one-seventh of that value. Was this depreciated paper freely accepted? No. The Government offered that or nothing. The relation of the individual to the Government, and the circumstances of the offer, rendered the acceptance a forced, not a free one. The same degree of constraint would vitiate a transaction between man and man before any Court of Equity on the face of the earth. There are even cases where consent cannot be pretended; where the property of the planter or farmer had been taken at the point of the bayonet, and a certificate presented in the same manner. But why did the creditors part with their acknowledgment of the debt? In some instances, from necessity; in others, from a well-founded distrust of the public. Whether from the one or the other, they had been injured; they had suffered loss, through the default of the debtor; and the debtor cannot, in justice or honor, take advantage of the default.

Here, then, was a debt acknowledged to have been once due, and which was never discharged; because the payment was forced and defective. The balance, consequently, is still due, and is of as sacred a nature as the claims of the purchasing holder can be; and if both are not to be paid in the whole, is equally entitled to payment in part. He begged gentlemen would not yield too readily to the artificial niceties of forensic reasoning; that they would consider not the form, but the substance — not the letter, but the equity — not the bark, but the pith of the business. It was a great and an extraordinary case; it ought to be

decided on the great and fundamental principles of justice. He had been animadverted upon for appealing to the heart as well as the head: he would be bold, nevertheless, to repeat, that, in great and unusual questions of morality, the heart is the best judge.

* * *

The proposition had been charged with robbing one set of men to pay another. If there were robbery in the case, it had been committed on the original creditors. But, to speak more accurately, as well as more moderately, the proposition would do no more than withhold a part from each of two creditors, where both were not to be paid the whole.

* * *

Objections to the measure had been drawn from its supposed tendency to impede public credit. He thought it, on the contrary, perfectly consistent with the establishment of public credit. It was in vain to say, that Government ought never to revise measures once decided. Great caution on this head ought, no doubt, to be observed: but there were situations in which, without some Legislative interposition, the first principles of justice, and the very ends of civil society, would be frustrated. The gentlemen themselves had been compelled to make exceptions to the general doctrine: they would probably make more before the business was at an end.

* * *

The best source of confidence in Government was the apparent honesty of its views. The proposition could not possibly be ascribed to any other motive than this, because the public was not to gain a farthing by it. The next source was an experienced punctuality in the payments due from the Government. For this support to public credit, he relied on what had been experienced by a part of the foreign creditors; on the provision to be made for the residue; and on the punctuality which, he flattered himself, would be observed in all future payments of the domestic creditors. He was more apprehensive of injury to public credit from such modifications of the interest of the public debt as some gentlemen seemed to have in view. In these the public would be the gainer, and the plea of inability the more alarming, because it was so easy to set up, so difficult to be disproved, and for which, consequently, the temptations would be so alluring.

The impracticability of the measure was the remaining ground on which it had been attacked. He did not deny that it would be attended with difficulties, and that perfect justice would not be done. But these were not the questions. It was sufficient that a grievous injustice would be lessened, and that the difficulties might be surmounted. What he had in view was, that for the conveniency of claimants some authority should be provided, and properly distributed through the Union, in order to investigate and ascertain the claims; and that, for the security of the public, the burden of proof should be thrown on the claimants. A scrutiny on this plan, aided by original settlements in the books of the army department, and the State commissioners, and other office documents, would be a remedy, at once, for all the difficulties stated with regard to fictitious names, certificates issued as money by commissaries and quartermasters, due bills, &c.

For some particular cases, special provisions might be requisite. . . .

The danger of frauds and perjuries had been worked up into a formidable objection. If these had always been equally alarming, no provision could ever have been made for the settlement or discharge of public debts. He reminded the committee of the frauds and perjuries for which a door had been opened by the final settlements, &c., of the frauds and perjuries inseparable from the collection of imposts and excises; yet these were all submitted to as necessary evils, because justice could not be done without them. The frauds and perjuries incident to this supplementary provision for justice must be very inconsiderable in number; and still more so, when compared either with the object to be obtained, or with the like evils already encountered in pursuit of a like object.

Great ingenuity and information had been exerted by the gentlemen on the other side in raising difficulties. He was sure that, after an adoption of the proposition, the same exertion would be used in removing them, and with such aid, the idea of impracticability would vanish.

ELBRIDGE GERRY,[3] *Massachusetts.*

(February 18, 1790)

It is admitted on all sides that the preservation of public faith is indispensable to the welfare of the Union, and in what does it consist? Public faith, as I conceive, consists in a punctual fulfillment of engagements and contracts on the part of Government. To preserve public faith, therefore, it is necessary that a nation should have adequate resources, the Government adequate powers, and those who administer it integrity and abilities. That our resources are equal to the payment of our debts, had not been denied; that Congress have not sufficient power, I presume none will assert.

[3] Though later (1812) elected to the Vice Presidency of the United States as a Jeffersonian, he was at this time a strong supporter of Hamiltonian policies and deeply interested in the market for public securities.

The preservation, then, of public faith will principally depend on their integrity and abilities. Their abilities may not be questioned, but their conduct in this case will be critically examined, and tried by the standard of morality. If it will stand the test, they will have the confidence of the people; but if not, vain will be every attempt to establish public credit. For this is nothing but the confidence of the people in public faith, and the people will think that, whatever resources they may have, or power to change the form of Government, the defective principles of the rulers can only be corrected by the Sovereign of the Universe. Is it good policy, then, to rest the public faith on an act of discrimination, which is intended to saddle one class of citizens with a tax to repair the loss which another class has sustained by a breach of contract on the part of the public? This will wear the appearance of committing one fraud to cure another. The right of speculators to purchase certificates at the market price is undoubted, and their conduct in making the purchases and payments is unexceptionable; but if there was a doubt of this in regard to some, would it be a sufficient ground for a discrimination?

SAMUEL LIVERMORE, *New Hampshire.*
(February 19, 1790)

Mr. Livermore said he was against any discrimination between the soldier and other public creditor who held a public security, made payable to bearer, and consequently transferable, with intent that they might be sold, if convenience or necessity should require it. This had been understood by all parties, as well in America as in foreign countries, and they had been sold accordingly. The advocates for discrimination have not denied this; they have only alleged that the low rate at which the poor soldier or other public creditor had sold his securities was a sufficient reason for Congress to interfere and set aside the sale. In opposition to this, he observed, that persons had a right to buy and sell at such prices as they could mutually agree upon, provided there was no fraud.

A diamond, a horse, or a lot of ground, might be sold too cheap or too dear, and so might any other property; but Government could not interfere without destroying the general system of law and justice. Esau had sold his birthright for a mess of pottage, and heaven and earth had confirmed the sale. The distresses of the army, both officers and soldiers, at the time they received and sold their securities, had been painted in too strong colors. They were not so emaciated by sickness and famine as had been represented. They were crowned with victory, and received with applause by their fellow-citizens: and although they had been paid in paper, their loss had been made up by large bounties, and in other emoluments; so that, in point of property, they were equal to their fellow-citizens, who had borne the burden of taxes under which many are laboring to this day. Let them be called brave soldiers, patriotic soldiers, but not poor soldiers. They ought to be governed by the same system of justice that governs others; but their contracts ought not to be set aside out of partiality to them.

JAMES MADISON, *Virginia.*
(February 19, 1790)

If paper, or the honor of statues or medals, can discharge the debts of justice, payable in gold or silver, we cannot only exonerate ourselves from those due to the original holders, but from those of the assignees; so far as paper goes the latter have received the compensation.

If honor can discharge the debt, they have received civil honors; look round to the officers of every Government in the Union, and you find them sharing equal honors with those bestowed on the original creditors. But, sir, the debt due in gold and silver is not payable either in honor, appointments, or in paper.

Gentlemen say it will work injustice; but are we not as much bound to repair the injustice done by the United States? Yet I do not believe the assertion has been established by any thing that has been urged in its support. The gentleman from Maryland (Mr. Stone), acknowledges that there is a moral obligation to compensate the original holders; how will they get what he admits is their due? He is willing to make an effort by applying the resources of the country to that purpose; but if we are to judge by the sentiments of other gentlemen who have spoken on this occasion, we have little to expect from that quarter. Suppose the debt had depreciated to a mere trifle, and suppose the sale of the Western Territory had extinguished the certificates, let me ask, whether, if the United States had thus exonerated themselves from the

obligation to the assignee, whether the claim of the original holder would not still remain in its full force in a moral view? But believing the point of justice to be exhausted, I will just add one remark upon the practicability. The transferred certificates, generally, will show the names of the original holders, and here there is no difficulty. With respect to those granted to the heads of either of the five great departments, the books of the Treasurer of Loans, as well as the accounts of those departments now in the Treasury, will designate with a great degree of accuracy, and this may be followed up by the usual mode of obtaining evidence; and I believe, every security may be provided against fraud in this case that was provided in the case of the commissioners who were sent into the respective States for ascertaining and liquidating the claims of individuals. That there will be some difficulty I admit, but it is enough for me that it is not insuperable; and I trust, with the assistance which the cause of equity and justice will ever obtain from the members of the National Legislature, they will easily be surmounted.

ASSUMPTION OF STATE DEBTS

James Madison, *Virginia.*

(April 22, 1790)

... The debts of the particular States cannot, in any point of view, be considered as actual debts of the United States; and the United States are not bound, by any past requisition, or any resolutions now existing, to assume them, till the accounts are settled and the balances ascertained. We have been told, sir, not only that the assumption of the State debts, by the United States, is a matter of right on the part of the States, and a

matter of obligation on the part of the United States, but likewise that it is equitable; nay, that it is a matter of necessity.

It has been said, that the United States are invested with the resources of the particular States, and that therefore they are bound to provide for the debts of those States. I think I may safely rest the issue of this question on a question of fact, Whether the States most urgent in this business are incapacitated from providing for their debts by the establishment of the present Constitution? If gentlemen assert that to be the case, I think it is incumbent upon them to prove, either that the resources which they have given up would exceed their quota of the Federal requisitions, or that the use of these resources by the General Government will throw a disproportioned burden upon that particular part of the community. Let us consider, sir, what is the ratio in which the States, in their individual capacity, ought to bear the debts of the United States, and what is the ratio in which they will contribute under the taxes that it is proposed to levy. The only evidence by which we can guide ourselves in this inquiry, is a statement from the several custom-houses. I believe, indeed, that such a statement may not be conclusive. I think it is imperfect; at the same time it is the best guide in our reach, and probably it will be sufficient to illustrate the present argument. The State of New Hampshire, according to this statement, will contribute about one hundredth part of what will be contributed by the whole. Her ratio of contribution, according to her representation, would be nearly about one-twentieth. Here, then, in fact, is a saving of four-fifths to that State. The State may then take this saving, and apply it to the purpose of discharging her domestic debt; she is relieved in that proportion, and therefore, in that proportion she is more able to provide for her State debt under the new Constitution than under the old one.

The State of Connecticut will contribute about one thirty-eighth; her proper quota would be about one-thirteenth. Here, then, is a saving of two-thirds to the State of Connecticut; and in that proportion is her situation better under the new Constitution than the old. Taking the States eastward of

New York altogether, that the gentlemen say are rendered incapable of bearing the burden of the State debts, by the adoption of the new Constitution; I say, take the whole together, and they will contribute about a sixth only; whereas they would have had to contribute a fourth if this Constitution had not been established, and they had paid their part of the debt of the United States. In my apprehension, then, sir, as the payment of the State debts cannot be claimed as a matter of right, neither can such payment be called for on the principles of equity, or, what is most of all urged, necessity. But we are told, that policy is also in favor of the measure. A gentleman from Massachusetts has said, that the people of Massachusetts never would submit to a rejection of the measure; that it will create a spirit of opposition to the Government; in short, that it will endanger the Union itself. I confess that these are consequences that would be dreadful to me if I could suppose they would really take place, and that evils of greater magnitude would not ensue from an adoption of the measure. It is my opinion, sir, that if the refusal to assume the State debts would produce dangerous consequences to the Union, from the discontents that it is apprehended will grow out of the measure, much more have we to fear from an assumption, particularly if hazarded by a small majority. Sir, if we could ascertain the opinions of our constituents, individually, I believe we should find four-fifths of the citizens of the United States against the assumption. I believe we should find more. I believe I speak within bounds when I say, that those who would be for an assumption would not amount to one-fifth. This is, indeed, probable conjecture only. But on the other hand, let me ask, what evidence

have we that there will be any great disappointment or discontents from a non-
assumption? The Legislature of the State
of New Hampshire have lately been in
session; have they asked for this assumption? No; on the contrary, though they
have not instructed their delegates to
vote against it, it appears that it was
thought of, and that the bulk of the
members disapproved of it. The Legislature of Massachusetts have been in session; they were apprised that this matter
was under consideration, and yet there
has been no declaration from them, as far
as I know, that can induce us to believe
they wish for it; on the contrary, it would
appear, from the measures they have
taken to provide for the payment of their
State debt, that they had proceeded on a
supposition that an assumption would
not take place. With respect to several
other States, their Legislatures have also
been in session, and none of them, except
South Carolina, have made any declaration on the subject. If we are to dis-
regard that species of evidence, and to
look back to the expectations of the
people, I do not think that there is a
single indication that this measure was
ever thought of by our constituents. Sir,
I may safely say, it was never expected
by the generality of them.

It has been said, too, that policy rec-
ommends the measure. It has been repeated, that if the assumption does not
take place, no part of the revenues drawn
from the Union at large will return to
the distant parts of it. Sir, I thought this
argument had been set aside some time
since. The very reverse will happen. The
State debts have begun already to travel
towards the central parts of the Union,
and to such an amount as to make it
probable, that if they are provided for
by us, nearly the whole will follow.
Should this be the case, I believe such

disadvantages will ensue as will prove
the measure very impolitic. In proportion as the whole money contributed
in the way of taxes shall centre near the
Government, or in a particular part of
the Union, you increase the evil of dis-
cordant interests and local jealousies,
which is already too much felt. But, perhaps, this is not the worst consequence
to be apprehended. I conceive that a
very great part of the proper debt of the
United States will go into the hands of
foreigners, and that we shall be heavily
burdened in paying an interest to them,
which cannot be expected to remain in
the country; and in proportion as you
increase the debt of the United States,
you will increase this evil.

I am of opinion, also, that the measure
is not politic, because, if the public debt
is a public evil, an assumption of the
State debts will enormously increase,
and, perhaps, perpetuate it. It is my idea,
sir, that the United States and the several
States could discharge a debt of eighty
millions, with greater ease, and in less
time, than the United States alone could
do it. I found my opinion on this consideration, that after the United States
shall have resorted to every means of
taxation within their power, there will
still remain resources from which moneys
may be raised by the States. Nay, I will
go further, and illustrate the remark by
adding, that after a State shall have extended its power of taxation to every
object falling under general laws, there
would still remain resources from which
further taxes might be drawn within sub-
divisions of it, by the subordinate authorities of the State. But, sir, when we consider, that in some parts of the Union
there is an unconquerable aversion to
direct taxes, at least if laid by the General Government; that in other parts an
equal aversion to excises prevails; how

will the United States, so circumscribed as to the field of taxation, be able to draw forth such resources as are contemplated by the advocates of an assumption?

It has been asserted that it would be politic to assume the State debts, because it would add strength to the National Government. There is no man more anxious for the success of the Government than I am, and no one who will join more heartily in curing its defects; but I wish these defects to be remedied by additional constitutional powers, if they should be found necessary. This is the only proper, effectual, and permanent remedy.

* * *

Much has been said of the situation of particular States, in case these debts should not be assumed. Much, indeed, has been said of the distresses and exertions of Massachusetts; but if we are to be governed by inquiries of this sort, we must extend them to every part of the Union, and we shall then find that an assumption will give as much dissatisfaction and work as much injustice to a majority of the States, as a non-assumption may disappoint the citizens of Massachusetts. I do not wish to go into local inquiries; but the present subject seems, in its nature, to make them in some degree unavoidable. The conduct of gentlemen on the other side, at least, renders the task on this indispensable. What would be the operation of the measure with respect to Virginia? It will not be denied, that Virginia sacrificed as much during the war, in one shape or other, and contributed as much to the common defence of the States, as any among them, certainly as much as Massachusetts. These are facts that can in time be proved. Since the peace, that State has made great exertions to comply with the requisitions of Congress. I might say, sir, that she was almost unequalled in her exertions. Her specie payments into the Federal Treasury since the peace, exceed six hundred thousand dollars, whereas those of Massachusetts are only between two and three hundred thousand dollars. In indents Massachusetts has, indeed, paid most, but by no means in such proportion as to balance the difference in the specie payments. The exertions of Virginia to discharge the debt she involved herself in by the war, have also been very great; she is not behind any of the States, she is before most of them; there can be no doubt but that she has certainly discharged more of her debts than Massachusetts, and as little doubt, in the opinion of the best informed, that whenever a final settlement shall take place, that State will be found a creditor to the United States.

If, during the war, she has made as great exertions, and has suffered as much as any of the States; if she has, since the peace, paid her full proportion of the supplies to the Federal Treasury, at the same time exerting herself to the utmost to discharge her State debt, and if, finally, she will probably be found to be in advance to the Union, and would, therefore, if justice could at once be done, be now entitled to a reimbursement — what must be said by the citizens of that State, if, instead of reimbursement, they are called upon to make further advances? Sir, I may add here, that their contributions to the Federal Treasury, under the proposed system of revenue, will exceed the ratio by which they would contribute, by taxes laid in proportion to their representation. I do not wish to extend this investigation any further than has been already done; but were I to do it, the evidence would be more striking, that the payments from those parts of the Union that would receive least benefit from the assumption, would be greater than from those that would receive the immediate benefit of it.

One of my colleagues seems to be of opinion, that the measure will be favorable to the interest of Virginia; but he seems to me to have grounded his opinion on the erroneous supposition that the proposed plan will embrace the whole of the debts as they existed at the close of the war, or that the State of Virginia will contribute less, on the plan of deriving revenue from consumption, than she would if derived according to the constitutional ratio. I believe, on the contrary, that if the assumption should take place as originally proposed, that there would be a claim on Virginia for five miillions, whereas, if there is no assumption, her citizens will have to provide for about three millions only; and thus, instead of bearing her proper burden, which is about one-seventh, she would have to bear a burden in the ratio of one-fifth. . . . But the citizens of Virginia would not only be called upon when already in advance, and to an amount beyond their proper ratio, but in a mode that is peculiarly obnoxious to them. I mean that of excise. Sir, the people of that State are as averse to excises as those of any other State can be to direct taxes, and in my own judgment, with far more reason, where the article excised is not by some peculiarity free from the common objections. Excises are unequal with respect to different parts of the Union. They are also unequal to various parts of the same State. This mode of collection gives arbitrary powers to the collectors, and exposes our citizens to vexatious searches. It opens a door to frauds and perjuries, that tend equally to vitiate the morals of the people, and to defeat the public

revenue. Besides, sir, excises are more expensive in the collection than other kinds of taxes. . . .

. . . . Let us take a view, comparatively, of the people of the United States. Massachusetts owes a debt of several millions. The public debt, when you come to analyze it, at least where it is due to citizens and not to foreigners, is a debt from one part of the people to the other. The Government is the collector from the pockets of the debtors, to pay it into the hands of the creditors. If, sir, the State debts should be assumed, Massachusetts will then get rid of her embarrassments; but what would be the situation of Virginia? Besides her public debt, I believe that her citizens owe, one to another, debts to an amount equal to the whole public debt of Massachusetts. Perhaps, I might say, to the amount of both the public and private debts of that State. In addition to all this, the people of Virginia are indebted to foreigners to a greater amount than the whole debt of Massachusetts. Sir, I firmly believe, that though Virginia is less oppressed with public debt than Massachusetts, yet, when we take a view of all the difficulties she labors under, and weigh them against those of Massachusetts, it will be found that Virginia ought to be relieved herself, instead of being expected to relieve others.

*   *   *

I cannot finish my observations on this subject, sir, without adverting to one particular, which I would wish gentlemen to attend to, not so much for our sakes as their own. I would recommend to them no longer to assume a pre-eminence over us in the nationality of their motives; and that they would forbear those frequent assertions, that if the State debts are not provided for, the Federal debts shall also go unprovided for; nay, that if the State debts are not assumed, the Union will be endangered. Sir, I am persuaded that if the gentlemen knew the motives which govern us, they would blush at such intemperate as well as inconsistent language. I am sure, that if they knew the emotions with which it is heard, they would at least see the inutility of it. I hope, sir, that whatever may be the decision on this question of assumption, that patriotism and every other noble and generous motive will lead the minority to acquiesce in measures which will tend to establish public credit by a due provision for the public engagements.

FISHER AMES, *Massachusetts.*
(May 25, 1790)
. . . I . . . ask whether, if the war had been confined to a corner, instead of spreading over the Continent, and one State had incurred the whole debt of eighty millions, it would be just to leave the burden upon that State? Consistently with the resolves I have mentioned, and the known sense of America, could it be called a State debt? I am sure of my answer, for the question extorts it. The difference between the case I have supposed, and that which is in debate, is only in degree — there is none in the principle.

*   *   *

The States were called upon during the war to make advances. Accordingly, they procured something by taxes, and still more was procured by paper money, which died in the hands of the possessor. They have also paid some part since the peace. So far the States, as such, actually made advances; but the principal part was obtained either by borrowing, or seizing private property, or draughting men. So far the advances were made by individuals, and at periods so critical, and

under such circumstances of violence and hardship, as to give a peculiar sanction to their claim upon the justice and honor of their country.

Justice plainly requires that these persons should be repaid their interest at least, in all events, and without delay. Their claims, in every view, are perfect; most of them are original holders. But neither the justice of the case, nor the engagements of Congress, require that the States should be repaid until the extent of their demand can be known. For I readily admit, that nothing more than the balances of their actual advances are due from the United States to the individual States. This has been urged against the assumption, but without foundation. If a State paid more than its proper share, the surplus should be repaid. But if a payment was only promised, and is still to be made, justice is due to the creditors and not to the State. The idea may be illustrated by considering the States as agents or contractors for the Union; what they paid, they claimed for themselves; what they barely promised should be paid, by their employers, who had the benefit of the debt, especially if the agent cannot or will not pay. I cannot think it necessary to give any further answer to the question so logically proposed with regard to the nature of the debts when redeemed, and in the State treasuries.

What remains due ought to fall not unequally upon States, but upon the whole society. It ought, if not paid sooner, to fall upon posterity. If some States should lose wealth and people, and other increase, if new States should join the Union, or spring up within it, and the Western wilderness be thronged with people, the burden will be equalized upon all the citizens. Liberty and independence were procured for the whole, and for posterity; why then should not all contribute to the price?

*　*　*

The best fund of the States, and hitherto the only one of the Union, the impost, has been taken away by adopting the Constitution. Let the debts follow the funds. Let the world judge whether the generous confidence of the State creditors in the justice ought to be abused, and whether they ought to be made to repent the cordial support which they gave to the new Constitution. The force of this argument may be inferred from the uncommon pains which have been taken to destroy it. The fact is denied, and the issue of the question has been boldly rested upon this point, that the States most urgent for the assumption were not incapacitated from providing for their debts by the surrender of the impost. The impost collected in New Hampshire is called the amount of that State's contribution to the Union, and the ratio by which she ought to contribute is taken from her present representation. I waive, at this moment, all comment upon the unfairness and fallacy of this mode of computation. I proceed to observe that an uncommon use is made of the result. According to her number of representatives, that State ought to pay one-twentieth, and yet no more than a hundredth part of the impost of the Union is paid by that State, or rather collected in it; of course, it is gravely said, it will save four-fifths of the sum which it would have had to pay if the debt had been assessed upon the Union before the Constitution was framed, and this saving to the State may apply to the discharge of its debt. But, sir, such requisitions never were paid, and never could have been paid by the State. Experience had taught us that it was not

to be expected, nor was it in their power. This, indeed, was one of the principal reasons for adopting the Constitution. Are we seriously addressed when we are told that the savings of a revenue, which did not exist, that four-fifths of nothing, may be applied to pay the State creditors? Without further regarding the ridicule of the argument, let us trace the fact. The debt of New Hampshire is said to be about 230,000 dollars; the yearly interest at four per cent, is upwards of 9,000 dollars. The impost and tonnage collected in that State, from August to December, is near 8,000 dollars. So that the impost of that State, though far short of her actual contribution to the common Treasury, will, in the whole year, greatly exceed their interest, which assuming her debt will throw upon the United States. Here, then, the fund surrendered by that State is more than adequate to the debt which ought to follow it. The whole cause has been hazarded on the fact, and here the fact is against him who appealed to it. May I be permitted to ask, whether it is not to be lamented, that through inadvertency or mistake, the whole was not mentioned? May I demand why the non-importing States were preferred to the importing States for calculating the impost? Massachusetts collected, under a State law, near 150,000 dollars impost yearly. This falls short of her present collection under the law of the Union, which is nearly equal to the interest of her debt. The excise would have supplied the deficiency, and that fund you are about to invade. It would be wrong to take away funds, though inferior to the discharge of interest, and yet to leave the whole debt upon the State. If the funds surrendered were equal to the debts, it has been admitted that the Union ought to take the debts also. The injustice of rejecting the debts, and taking the impost to a less amount, differs only in degree. But why was New York passed over in silence? The interest of the debt of that Sate would not equal the impost collected within it. What will you say to that State?

The candor and impartiality of the committee will be exercised in deciding whether the arguments so often urged in favor of the assumption, that you ought to take the debts with the impost, has lost any thing of its force by this investigation of facts. What is asserted on one side, and denied on the other, after a strict inquiry, ends in the same point.

There is another view of the subject to be taken. It is allowed that the people pay duties in proportion as they consume duted articles. The consumption in the several States is nearly according to the numbers of the people. It will be as fair in this as in the former calculation, to take the number of representatives as our rule to compute the proportions which the several States contribute by the consumption of articles charged with duties. The impost of New Hampshire and Massachusetts, collected within the period from August to December, and added together, was nearly one hundred and twenty thousand dollars. Allow the former three parts in eleven, according to her representation, and it will appear that her citizens paid thirty-two thousand seven hundred dollars of the whole sum. Less than eight thousand dollars were collected within the State. In case the debts should not be assumed, but should be provided for by State duties and excises, according to these principles, the citizens of New Hampshire would have to pay five thousand dollars a month, or at the rate of twenty-five thousand dollars from August to December, into the treasury of Massachusetts. Connecticut in like manner would pay within an equal

period fifty-four thousand dollars, and Jersey, if reckoned with New York, would have to pay about sixty thousand dollars, and with Pennsylvania still more. In a whole year, this tribute which one State would exact from another would amount to very large sums. North Carolina is a non-importing State, and in common with the others before mentioned, would have to pay for the debt of its neighbors, and then to provide for its own. Is there any injustice or cause of discord or violence charged, or even imagined against the assumption equal to this? And yet we hear it said, let us leave the States to pay their debts for themselves.

*   *   *

This measure can neither increase nor diminish the power of the Government; for the power to be exercised is expressly given it by the Constitution. Will it embarrass the exercise of power? The contrary is true; it removes impediments which will be in its way, if not assumed. Experience has taught us, to our cost, how very pernicious those obstacles are. The systems of State revenues, before the Constitution was formed, had crushed industry and almost ruined trade from State to State.

Will its tendency be to evil rather than to common benefit? This, it is true, is a vague as well as complex question; but its great objects are to establish justice; to produce equality of burdens and benefits, an uniform revenue system; to secure public credit by removing every example of bad faith, and to prevent all interference between the National and State Governments, and the dangerous usurpation of the one upon the other, which would be the consequence.

How can it be said that policy is against the measure, if its tendency be such? Much has been said about consolidation. Certainly it cannot be usurpation for Congress to pay the debts which were contracted either by itself, or, at its own request, by the States. The State Governments are said to be in danger of a consolidation: that, however, is not the only, probably not the greatest, danger they have to risk; disunion is still more formidable. Nothing can shelter the small States from the greater ones but union; nor would any single State be safe against the combination of several States. All would be exposed to foreign foes. If you make the State Governments strong by taking strength from the Union, they become exposed exactly in the degree you do it. For the principle of union ought to be strong in proportion to the strength of the members. In a compound ratio, therefore, you make the National Government too weak to combine the whole together, and you expose Governments and citizens to the caprice of accidents and to the fury of passions, which will confound laws, liberty, and Governments.

It is true, a body of valuable citizens will be attached to the Government; all good citizens should love the Government, and they will do so, if Government should deserve their love. Revenue powers are given to Congress without reserve. To say that it is dangerous and improper to exercise them is a charge against the Constitution.

There are but three points of view to consider the State Governments in. Either as rivals for power, as watchmen, or as legislators within the State. To call them rivals would be an avowal of the principle of disunion, or rather of positive force, which is absurd. I do not know that either the State or National Constitutions have given them the office to watch this Government. The people are to watch us all, and I wish they always may. But if the State Governments are still called watchmen, that office may be performed as well, perhaps better, without than with the incumbrance of their debts. It is equally difficult to see how it can impair the rights of internal legislation. The assumption and an uniform plan of revenue will take away not only all pretext, but every motive for encroachment upon them. If, by the non-assumption, an interference is produced, their danger will be the more imminent. For, if they prevail in the conflict, they will be ruined by disunion; if they fail, they will be swallowed up in the consolidation. I wish, among other reasons, to have the assumption take place, because I think it will give us the best security that our Government will be administered as it was made, without suffering or making encroachments.

I hasten to notice some objections: a public debt is called an evil, and the assumption is charged with tending to increase and perpetuate it. I am not disposed to dispute about words, though I believe the debt, as a bond of union, will compensate the burden of providing for it. But I cannot admit that it is a greater evil to owe a debt, than to wipe it off without paying it; and if the whole debt is to be paid, at all events the assumption makes no increase; nay, if the modification first proposed should be made, the capital will be diminished near thirteen millions by this measure. It is said to be easier to pay eighty millions by leaving the State debts to be paid by the States, and paying the other debt ourselves, than to form the whole into one debt.

By this division of the debt, if there is any force in the objection, that we can pay more, or we shall pay what may be collected more easily, first, let us see whether this is true as to what the States will have to provide for. As it respects South Carolina, the contrary is confessedly true. So far is it from being a more easy way of paying, that they cannot pay at all. If Massachusetts can pay her interest, it will be with extreme difficulty. One gentleman observed that her efforts had raised a rebellion. It is certain that they have not succeeded. The price of the State paper in most of the States has been some proof of their incapacity to make effectual provision.

The State debts are to be paid, or they are not. If, by leaving them upon the States, they will be lost to the creditors, that cannot be supposed to be the most convenient mode of paying part of eighty millions, which is intended by the argument. Besides the shock to public credit, it would be a loss of so much property. The disaster would probably be more felt than some of the greatest physical evils, such as inundation or blasting the earth for a time with barrenness. If then the debts are to be paid, by what means? The gentleman from Virginia has strongly reprobated excises. The States cannot touch the impost, what remains? Direct taxes only. This source will be soon exhausted. . . . Taxes on land have cost as much to collect as excises. In one of the States I am told that the collection has been estimated at thirty per cent. Experience, too, has proved that the States cannot pay their debts by direct taxes. It has been pushed to the utmost extent, and found insufficient.

The argument which has been urged by the gentleman from Virginia against excises, seems to exclude this mode of revenue; without it, the State debts cannot be provided for. The United States will be compelled to resort to it. It is absolutely necessary for drawing forth the resources of the country. As every man consumes, every man will contrib-

ute, including foreigners and transient people. Imposts cannot be carried far without defeating the collection. Duties on imported spirits would increase the use of home-made spirits, which cannot be reached without an excise. All taxes are in some degree unequal, but excises probably as little so as any. The rates are fixed, and very little is left to imposition and caprice. Besides every consumer taxes himself.

*   *   *

If you reject excises, you cannot have an adequate revenue; and if the States have also excises, the revenue will be impoverished and hazarded. For if an article can pay both duties, there is a loss to get but one, it might as well be collected throughout the United States as in one State; and if it cannot pay both, one or both treasuries will suffer for the loss. Besides, you incur a double expense in collecting them.

What revenues are left you if the excise is rejected? With such a slender sum you cannot offer new terms. The modification of the entire debt, as first proposed, makes a saving in the capital of almost thirteen millions. The debt to be assumed is about twenty-four. The interest on the difference, or on the real increase of debt by assuming, is less than five hundred thousand dollars yearly.

We depend upon two principles for the security of the revenues. One is that the trading people will not be disposed to offend, and the other is that all others will be inclined to watch and expose them if they should. Never was so popular a revenue system. But the violence to the just demands of the creditors, depriving them of the money they have been used to receive, and creating in the States an interest to have your collection fail, in order to make the State funds effectual, will produce a most disastrous change. It is setting men's interests as well as opinions against you. Nor will the landed interest have a different sentiment, for they will be murmuring under the load of direct taxes, and the more the State revenues can be improved by lessening the National, the less they will have to bear.

What reason is there, then, for asserting that more money can be obtained, and more easily, by several systems than by one? This bold assertion, which the sense of America would refute, if its experience had not done it already, is not true of imposts. . . .

Without adequate funds the States cannot propose to their creditors a modification of the debt. By the Constitution they are restrained from passing laws to impair contracts. The burden will rest upon the States, if not assumed, at six per cent; for without funds the creditors will not consent to take less; if assumed, upon Congress at four; is this the more easy way of paying part of eighty millions? It makes a difference of several millions against the public.

* * *

It is an unusual thing for a gentleman in a public assembly to assert, that four fifths of the people are of his way of thinking. This, however, has been done. It is not strange for persons to mistake their own opinion for that of the public. These fond prepossessions may be received instead of evidence, but they cannot weigh much against evidence. My information may have been less diligently sought, and less carefully examined than that gentleman's; but I have compared it with what has been gathered by my friends, and I declare that I believe four-fifths of the wise and worthy men, in a very wide extent of country, look with strong disapprobation upon the injustice,

and with anxious terror upon the impolicy of rejecting the State debts.

Little notice has been taken of an argument for the assumption, which, if just, is entitled to a great deal. I mean that which has been urged to show that it will strengthen the Government. The answer given is, that instead of pecuniary influence, new powers are wanting to the Constitution. This is not denying the argument, but asserting a proposition, which, if false, is to be disregarded, and if true, is not inconsistent with the point in question. So far from denying, it seems to admit the utility of the assumption, and asserts the utility of some other thing. Which other thing he has not explained, and if he had, it is probably unattainable, nor will its attainment, be it what it may, be prevented by the assumption. But before we ask for new powers on paper, let us exercise those which are actually vested in Congress. What will new powers avail us, if we suffer the Constitution to become a dead letter? What has dropped from the gentleman on this point amounts to an important concession. Little topics of objection sink to nothing when it is allowed that the assumption will strengthen the Government. Is the principle of union too strong? Do not all good men desire to make it perfect? What nation has more to hope from union, or to fear from disunion? Shall we make the Union less strong than the people have intended to make it, by adopting the Constitution? And do not all agree that the assumption is not a neutral measure? If its adoption will give strength to the Union, its rejection will have the contrary effect.

JAMES JACKSON, *Georgia.* (July 23, 1790)

The question of justice has been subservient to both sides of the House; but the great rules, the leading features of justice, have not been answered, if they have been attempted. Where, I again demand, is the justice of compelling a State which has taxed her citizens for the sinking of her debt, to pay another proportion, not of her own, but the debts of other States, which have made no exertions whatever?

If this assumption had taken place at the conclusion of the war, the principle would have been more just than at present, because then none of the States had made exertions to relieve themselves from debt, and they were nearer on an equality; but even then it would not have been on perfect terms of justice; the situations of the States, and their charges, were not the same.

* * *

I consider the State which made exertions, as I mentioned on a former day, to have paid off so much of its proportion of these debts, whether called the debts of the States, or the debts of the Union. If State debts, no State ought to pay the debts of other States; if they are the debts of the Union, then has the State which has exerted itself and paid off its own debt, contributed its proportion, and ought not to pay a second time.

. . . . Neither are those debts of the same nature with that of the United States. The same scrutinizing eye hath not pervaded the respective States. Some States, in expectation of being the pay-masters themselves, have dealt with a rigid parsimony; others have been as extravagantly liberal. Some have allowed regiments of officers to their militia without men, whilst others have reduced their officers to a grinding situation. Some have allowed large bounties and pay, as has been the case with some of the States who complain most, whilst others have

scarcely allowed bounty or pay at all. Many of the charges of individual States would be rejected; whilst others, which the States have rejected, would be allowed. The difference is very great, and clear as the day, and none but interested individuals can prevent discerning it.

* * *

The . . . argument is, that the measure is founded in good policy, as well as justice, as it will promote harmony among creditors and different States, attach them to the Government, and facilitate operations.

That it is not founded in justice I think has been pretty well shown. Its policy was clearly proved, at a former day, to have been a consolidation of the Government; and, sir, I believe, with it, a consolidation of the people's liberties. The object certainly was the absorbing the whole of the State powers within the vortex of the all-devouring General Government; seven years were we fighting to establish props for liberty, and in less than two years since the adoption of the Constitution are we trying to kick them all away, and he is the ablest politician, and the best man of the day, who can do most to destroy the child of liberty of his own raising. A friend, sir, to the State Governments, or the liberties of the people, is as much lost at the present day, as if he had belonged to the last century, and had a resurrection in the present age.

But, sir, if so much of this patriotism is lost near the seat of Government, let us not suppose that it is the case with the whole of the United States. The States will not tamely submit to a measure calculated to distress, and manifestly founded in injustice and the ruin of the State Governments. So far will it be from producing the harmony the gentleman has supposed, that I think I can venture to prophesy it will occasion discord, and generate rancor against the Union. For if it benefits one part of the United States it oppresses another. If it lulls the *Shays* of the North it will rouse the *Sullivans* of the South.

The more checks there are to any Government, the more free will its citizens be. The State powers are a most effectual and necessary check against encroachments from the Government of the Union. The assumption, by annihilating the powers of the State Governments, will prove a decisive and fatal stroke at that check.

*   *   *

The gentleman from Connecticut has noticed an argument respecting the ratio of contribution by impost, and has alluded to the Journal of Congress of the 29th of April, 1783, where, he says, it is clearly proved that the States contribute to impost according to the number of inhabitants. The gentleman from Massachusetts has likewise noticed this. I grant those gentlemen that the consumer pays, but I deny that the States pay agreeably to population — they contribute, sir, agreeably to habit. Connecticut manufactures a great deal, and she imports little. Georgia manufactures nothing, and imports everything. Therefore Georgia, although her population is not near so large, contributes more to the public Treasury by impost.

WILLIAM LOUGHTON SMITH, S. *Carolina.*
    (July 23, 1790)
As the assumption relates to the Government of the United States, there can be no doubt that viewing it as a federal question, it will be a measure which will contribute to the more durable union of the States and will greatly facilitate the collection of the revenue. It will be just

and politic: just, because the expenses were incurred in the common cause, and ought to be paid from the common treasury; and because Congress are exclusively possessed of the best resources of the country; politic, because the State systems of revenue will obstruct and injure the national system and impair the credit of the United States. These considerations should have weight with those who are specially appointed to administer this Government. In a great national question they should not suffer local considerations to warp their judgment, and influence a vote on which, perhaps, the very existence of the Union may depend. Will it be denied that there will be a clashing between the States on the subject of taxes and excises, that there will be heart-burnings on the part of the State creditors who will be left destitute while ample provision is made for the Continental creditors; that many of them will not only connive at frauds in the revenue, but will even promote them, to reduce the Continental creditor to a level with themselves; that smuggling, instead of being viewed as a crime against the Union, will be deemed an innocent act, and even popular; because those who think themselves abandoned by the Government will feel themselves justified in thwarting the collection of a revenue which is to be distributed with so partial a hand? Shall our creditor be ruined because he happened to be a citizen of a State distant from the residence of Congress, and receive State securities, while another, perhaps less meritorious (for he might not have been a voluntary creditor) will have the principal and interest of his debt well funded, and a comfortable subsistence provided for the remainder of his days? Shall the bare circumstance of a Continental commissioner not going into a distant State till a considerable time after the peace, to liquidate the claims of its citizens, deprive them of a compensation for their services, or a retribution for their property employed in the common cause? Or shall the sufferings of a State during the war be aggravated at the peace, by saddling her with the payment of the debt incurred for general purposes? When these reflections rush on the minds of the State creditors, would it be surprising that they should abhor a Government by which they shall be treated with such palpable injustice?

THE PEOPLE OPPOSE HAMILTON'S DEBT PLAN

A COMMUNICATION TO THE *PENNSYLVANIA GAZETTE*
January 27, 1790

MUCH has been said, we are told, by the Secretary of the Federal Treasury, in his report, in favor of the necessity of supporting *public credit*. But public credit cannot exist, at the expense of public and private *justice*. The Congress owe the balance of the certificates, above 2sh. 6d. in the pound, to their army. To gain a character, therefore, they commit a flagrant act of injustice. And with whom is this character to be gained? With Speculators, and British and Dutch Brokers. But with whom will it be lost? With their army, with the best whigs in the union, and with half the widows and orphans in the United States. But why do they attempt to restore their national character by *halves?* By redeeming their certificates at their nominal value, and not making up the losses sustained by widows and orphans by their paper money, they resemble a girl, who comes forward in a white sheet to do penance for a *second* bastard, without asking pardon of God and the congregation for her *first* breach of chastity. Pub-

lic credit, therefore, at the expence of public and private justice, is folly and wickedness. The words are mere jingle, calculated only to catch weak people. But further, the proposed funding system is grossly oppressive upon the poor soldiers and officers of the American army. They must all pay taxes, to raise their certificates to their full value in the hands of the purchasers of them. Now is this right? It certainly is not. For then, instead of being paid by the United States for their services, or for their limbs, they are brought in debt to them: That is, an officer received a certificate of £200 instead of £1000 from them, and pays perhaps half the balance in taxes, for the benefit of the man to whom he sold it. Such injustice and oppression may be coloured over with fine words; but there is a time coming, when the pen of history will detect and expose the folly of the arguments in favor of the proposed funding system, as well as the iniquity. Instead of disgracing our country, by treating our army with so much ingratitude and injustice, it would be far better to double the public debt, by paying the soldier and the Speculator the same sum.

The Congress under the old confederation, after having paid their army in depreciated paper money, made up to them the difference afterwards in what they called depreciation certificates. Shall the Congress under the new government deny them the same justice, by refusing to pay them the difference between two shillings and sixpence and twenty shillings? — Or shall they do worse — Shall they pay it to men who never earned it, and who have already received an interest on their purchases equal to the sum they cost them?

Should the balance still due to our army be paid to them, it would spread money through every county and township of the United States. If it is paid to the speculators, all the cash of the United States will soon center in our cities, and afterwards in England and Holland.

By the proposed funding system the interest of the original certificate holder is reduced to four per cent. Now is this just? — To take forty shillings a year from the just gains of one man, and add ten pounds a year to the unjust gains of another? — Is not this selling Justice — and the United States — at public vendue, to the highest bidder?

A FARMER

A COMMUNICATION TO THE *PENNSYLVANIA GAZETTE*
February 3, 1790

In a former paper I took notice of the injuries which the proposed funding system will do the soldiers and other original holders of certificates, by compelling them to pay taxes, in order to appreciate their certificates in the hands of quartermasters, speculators and foreigners. The Secretary of the treasury has declared in his report, that these people sold their certificates from choice, and not always from necessity. This I believe is true in a very few instances. A hungry creditor, a distressed family, or perhaps, in some instances, the want of a meal's victuals, drove most of them to the Brokers Offices, or compelled them to surrender up their certificates. Two cases of this kind I shall briefly relate. A merchant in the city of Philadelphia put £10,000 into the funds in 1777. In the year 1788 his British creditors called upon him for payment of some old debts. In vain he looked up to Congress to refund him the principal he loaned to them. He had their notes, but

they were *worth* only £2,500, and at that rate only his creditors received them from him. Now, is it just that the British creditor should receive from our government £10,000, instead of the £2,500, and the person from whom they were torn by the treaty of peace be abandoned to poverty, despair and death, by his country? Perhaps that very £10,000 fed the American army on the very day that General Gates captured General Burgoyne.

The other case I shall mention is, of a sick soldier, who sold his certificates of £69.7.0 for £3.0.11, to a rich speculator. He went to this speculator after he recovered, and offered to redeem his certificate — but he refused to give it up. Now, can it be right that this poor soldier, every time he sips his bohea tea, or tastes a particle of sugar, should pay a tax to raise £3.0.11 to £69.7.0 in the hands of this speculator?

Thus we see public credit (that much

hackneyed and prostituted phrase) must be established at the expence of national justice, gratitude and humanity.

The whole report of the *Secretary* (as he so often stiles himself) is so flimsy, and so full of absurdities, contradictions and impracticabilities, that it is to be hoped it will be voted out of Congress without a dissenting voice.

It would be well enough to ask this Mr. Secretary, whether his friends have *bought* or sold most certificates? He has shewn that he does not believe in his own phantastical idea of national honor, or he never would have dared to reduce the interest on the original certificates to 4 per cent. If the nation is unable to pay the whole, then do justice. Pay the original holders 6 per cent agreeably to contract, and the purchaser 3 per cent. Here is justice done to one part of the creditors, and no injury to the other. On the contrary, a generous compensation is given to them for lying out of their money.

The following consequences will follow the adoption of the proposed funding system.

It will draw all the cash from the country to our cities, from whence it will be exported to England and Holland, to pay the annual interest of our greatly oppressive debt.

It will render it impossible for the farmers to borrow money to improve their lands, for who will lend money to an individual for 6 per cent when government securities will yield 8 and 12 per cent?

It will check trade and manufactures.

It will fill our country with brokers and idle speculators.

It will produce a principal of £200,000 to a few Nabobs in each of the states, who will sell this principal after a while to foreigners, and lay it out in buying townships and counties, to be cultivated by tenants who will administer to the ambition and power of these nabobs, and thereby enable them to establish titles, &c. and to overthrow the liberties of our country.

Would it not be proper for the farmers to unite immediately, and remonstrate against all these evils. They never were in half the danger of being ruined by the British government, that they now are by their own.

Had any person told them in the beginning of the war, that, after paying the yearly rent of their farms for seven years to carry on this war, at the close of it their farms should not be worth more than one fourth of their original cost and value, in consequence of a funding system — is there a farmer that would have embarked in the war? No, there is not. Why then should we be deceived, duped, defrauded and ruined by our new rulers? Let us do justice to our brave officers and soldiers. Great Britain paid the tories for their loyalty, although they did her cause more harm than good. Certainly the United States should not have less gratitude to her most deserving citizens, than Great Britain has shewn to her least deserving subjects.

A FARMER

Germantown, January 30.

A MEMORIAL FROM THE GENERAL ASSEMBLY OF VIRGINIA

IN THE HOUSE OF DELEGATES, *Thursday, the 16th of December, 1790.*

The General Assembly of the Commonwealth of Virginia to the United States in Congress assembled, represent:

That it is with great concern they find themselves compelled, from a sense of duty, to call the attention of Congress to an act of their last session, entitled "An act making provision for the debt of the United States," which the General Assembly conceives neither policy, justice, nor the constitution, warrants. Republican policy, in the opinion of your memorialists, could scarcely have suggested those clauses in the aforesaid act, which limit the right of the United States, in their redemption of the public debt. On the contrary, they discern a striking resemblance between this system and that which was introduced into England at the Revolution — a system which has perpetuated upon that nation an enormous debt, and has, moreover, insinuated into the hands of the Executive an unbounded influence, which, pervading every branch of the Government, bears down all opposition, and daily threatens the destruction of every thing that appertains to English liberty. The same causes produce the same effects.

In an agricultural country like this, therefore, to erect and concentrate and perpetuate a large moneyed interest, is a measure which your memorialists apprehend must, in the course of human events, produce one or other of two evils; the prostration of agriculture at the feet of commerce, or a change in the present form of Federal Government, fatal to the existence of American liberty.

The General Assembly pass by various other parts of the said act, which they apprehend will have a dangerous and impolitic tendency, and proceed to shew the injustice of it, as it applies to this Commonwealth. It pledges the faith of the United States for the payment of certain debts due by the several States in the Union, contracted by them during the late war.

A large proportion of the debt thus contracted by this State has been already redeemed by the collection of heavy taxes levied on its citizens, and measures have been taken for the gradual payment of the balance, so as to afford the most certain prospect of extinguishing the whole at a period not very distant. But, by the operation of the aforesaid act, a heavy debt, and consequently heavy taxes, will be entailed on the citizens of this Commonwealth, from which they never can be relieved by all the efforts of the General Assembly, whilst any part of the debts contracted by any State in the American Union, and so assumed, shall remain unpaid: for it is with great anxiety your memorialists perceive, that the said act, without the smallest necessity, is calculated to extort from the General Assembly the power of taxing their own constituents for the payment of their own debts, in such a manner as would be best suited to their own ease and convenience.

Your memorialists cannot suppress their uneasiness at the discriminating preference which is given to the holders of the principal of the Continental debt, over the holders of the principal of the State debts, in those instances where States have made ample provision for the annual payment of the interest, and

Reprinted in *American State Papers: Finance,* I, 90–91.

where, of course, there can be no interest to compound with the principal; which happens to be the situation of this Commonwealth.

The continental creditors have preferences in other respects, which the General Assembly forbear to mention, satisfied that Congress must allow, that policy, justice, and the principles of public credit, abhor discriminations between fair creditors.

Your memorialists turn away from the impolicy and injustice of the said act, and view it in another light, in which, to them, it appears still more odious and deformed.

During the whole discussion of the federal constitution, by the convention of Virginia, your memorialists were taught to believe, "that every power not granted, was retained"; under this impression, and upon this positive condition, declared in the instrument of ratification, the said Government was adopted by the people of this Commonwealth; but your memorialists can find no clause in the constitution, authorizing Congress to assume debts of the States! As the guardians, then, of the rights and interests of their constituents; as sentinels placed by them over the ministers of the Federal Government, to shield it from their encroachments, or at least to sound the alarm when it is threatened with invasion; they can never reconcile it to their consciences silently to acquiesce in a measure which

violates that hallowed maxim — a maxim, on the truth and sacredness of which, the Federal Government depended for its adoption in this Commonwealth. But this injudicious act not only deserves the censure of the General Assembly, because it is not warranted by the constitution of the United States, but, because it is repugnant to an express provision of that constitution. This provision is, "that all debts contracted, and engagements entered into, before the adoption of this constitution, shall be as valid against the United States, under this constitution, as under the Confederation"; which amounts to a constitutional ratification of the contracts respecting the State debts in the situation in which they existed under the Confederation; and, resorting to that standard, there can be no doubt that, in the present question, the rights of States, as contracting parties with the United States, must be considered as sacred.

The General Assembly of the Commonwealth of Virginia confide so fully in the justice and wisdom of Congress, upon the present occasion, as to hope that they will revise and amend the aforesaid act generally, and repeal, in particular, so much of it as relates to the assumption of the State debts.

Teste. CHARLES HAY, *c.h.d.*
1790, *December 23.*
Agreed to by the Senate.
H. BROOKE, *s.c.*

JAMES THOMSON CALLENDER: SEDGWICK & CO. OR A KEY TO THE SIX PER CENT CABINET

We proceed to examine the nature and merit of the domestic debt, or what are commonly called *the certificates of the old soldiers.*

A great clamour has been raised, as to

the injustice endured by the continental army. They were compelled from poverty to sell the certificates which they had obtained for their arrears of pay; and they received a very reduced price from the purchasers. One reason for this prodigious discount was the uncertainty whether the new government would undertake to fund that paper, and give security for its payment. It is believed that this subject has never yet been placed in a just light, by any of the parties concerned. A new path remains to be struck out. The discussion, after every trial to condense it, requires considerable room. Attention is entreated, and more than a common degree of patience.

We begin by examining this highly important question, what degree of moral obligation lies on the people of America to pay this domestic debt, these twenty-one annual instalments of six millions of dollars each? The morality must not, however, be confounded with the *expediency*. They are two matters essentially distinct from each other. It may prove extremely prudent to pay a claim, though not entirely just; because the trouble of contending about the money, will perhaps exceed the worth of it.

When the business came originally before the congress of 1789, three different plans were suggested. The first proposed a new settlement of accounts, and aimed to annihilate the largest part of the debt.[1] But the new constitution had been, in a great measure, established by the influence and activity of traders in these certificates. They and their friends were superior in the legislature; and this scheme was rejected by a numerous majority.

A second proposal went on the ground of paying to the purchasers only the real value they had given for the certificates, and to give the difference between the half crown which they had debursed, and the twenty shillings which they claimed, to the original holders. Thus, when Wil-

liam Smith demanded five hundred dollars, as the arrears due to an old serjeant, the reply might have run thus: "You gave fifty dollars of money for these five hundred of paper. Here take your fifty silver dollars back again. We shall reserve the remaining four hundred and fifty for the man who shed his blood in earning them." This plan, also, was negatived.

The third proposal succeeded, and by it the whole debt was funded, at its full value of twenty shillings per pound, on behalf of the actual holders of the paper. The plan was, indeed, morally certain of being adopted; for a great number of members of congress had previously entered into a combination to purchase up certificates, because they knew that they would be strong enough, in both houses, to carry the vote for having them funded at full value. On these three projects, Mr. Gallatin has the following observations.

Whether the debt had been funded on the plan of discrimination, in favour of the original holders, of those who had performed the services, or, *as has been the case,* in favour of the purchasers of certificates, the general effects would have been nearly the same;[2] and unless the American government had chosen to forfeit every claim to common honesty, it must necessarily provide [*have provided*] for discharging the principal, or paying the interest, to one or the other of (*those*) two descriptions of persons.

[The first of the three plans above recited aimed at annihilating the greater part of this domestic debt. The words *every claim to common honesty* express a positive affirmation that the supporters of that project were void of honesty.]

[1] Gallatin, P. 97.

[2] By no means: the plan adopted has issued in erecting an oppressive, and paper-jobbing aristocracy. If divided among the original holders, the debt would have fostered a substantial and republican yeomanry. These two effects were as opposite as Elysium and Erebus.

Whatever difference of opinion may heretofore have existed on that subject, on the propriety of paying those who had purchased the debt *so much under its value,* it now exists no more. It has ceased with the cause; for all the present owners have, or may be *supposed to have* purchased the debt at the market price, which, since it has been funded, has been obtained for it. The solemn obligations, superadded by the *present government* [or, to speak plainly, by the *creditors themselves,*] to those contracted before, never can be set aside without the most flagrant and pernicious breach of public faith and of national morality.[3]

Our author sets out on this basis that there was a moral *wrong* in the primitive construction of the rights of these purchasers of certificates. He next assumes the as yet unheard of doctrine, that conveyance to a purchaser of good faith has the power of creating a just title to enforce a claim fraudulent in itself. This is precisely affirming that the *bona fide* indorsee of a forged bill is warranted to recover payment, because he truly and fairly advanced value for the indorsation. Whatever doubt was held about paying the congressional paper-jobber, his assignee certainly gave complete value for the six per cent stock. You *must* satisfy him. On the same ground, a swindler, or a footpad, has only to secure an honest transferree; and his plunder lies beyond the gripe of restitution. This maxim, if carried into practice, would dissolve and extinguish every tie which holds society together. A more absurd or pernicious doctrine was never pronounced. Mr. Gallatin could hardly be serious in believing his own affirmation. It is better to drop the pen, than to write what is evidently fabulous, and especially when the fiction is of such a nature as to undermine every safeguard of property.

3 Gallatin, P. 131.

To illustrate this topic, figure the case that a person at Pittsburg shall steal a horse from Mr. Gallatin, and shall bring him down to Philadelphia. The horse is there bought for government service. He is again sold to a second purchaser, who pays an honest price for him, and suspects no harm.

The new buyer sets out for the westward, and meets our legislator coming down to congress. Mr. Gallatin stops him by the bridle, claims the horse, and relates the robbery. "I have nothing to do with that," says the other, "I gave the full value. Here is a receipt for the money, subscribed by the treasurer of Pennsylvania. Since the horse was stolen he has passed through several hands. The solemn obligation superadded by the treasurer of the state to those contracted before, never can be set aside without the *most flagrant* and *pernicious breach of public faith,*" &c. as above.

Mr. Gallatin would not be satisfied with this answer. He would not think it the *most flagrant breach of morality* to take his own horse back again, and to leave the last purchaser to seek redress where he could find it. He would infallibly reclaim his property, though in the hands of a ten-thousandth *bona fide* purchaser. He would say that right can never be founded on wrong; that a thief can never convey a title to the fruits of roguery, because he has no title to himself. His plea would be confirmed by the civil law, by the common law, the natural sense of justice, and the usage of civilized nations. Every man must feel the rectitude of such a demand. No judge durst refuse to restore the horse.

This comparison comes tolerably close. The animal stolen represents a certificate for a thousand dollars of domestic debt. The culprit typifies a congress member, voting that the public shall pay to *himself*, six, twelve, or twenty four[4] times the value which he gave to the first holder for that certificate. The receipt by the treasurer is designed as the funding statute. The last buyer of the horse represents an honest unsuspecting purchaser from one of the funding majority, and who is ignorant, perhaps, that Hamilton, Sedgwick, or William Smith ever had a being.

Unless there be some clandestine edition of the decalogue, reserved for the peculiar service of government, the same rule applies to the rights of an individual, and to those of a nation. To the original holders of the debt, the United States may justly say that they have already received, in the shape of interest, more than they ever did actually disburse, with the compound interest of their advances collectively. Mr. Gallatin suspects, that there has been a deception in the foundation of the business. In that case, an honest assignee of six per cent stock may be told, that the whole transaction was fraudulent, that the United States were grossly betrayed by a legislative majority; and that, as a bond granted for a shameful cause, is, of itself, null and void in law, the same doctrine corresponds to public debt.

Mr. Alexander Hamilton grounds his late defence of his character upon his having had no pecuniary concern with the speculations in this funding system. He directly implies that he looked upon these legislators, as Mr. Gallatin, and the rest of mankind, have always looked upon them. If the affair had been honorable on the part of Congress members, it would have been equally so upon his part. He, and they, were alike trustees for the public at large. There is, indeed,

an apparent but trifling distinction between them. An act of Congress of September 2d, 1789, prohibits all persons holding an office in the treasury from being "concerned in the purchase or disposal of any public securities of any state, or of the United States." Disqualification, and a penalty of three thousand dollars, are to be the consequence of detection.

But if the injunction was requisite upon officers of the treasury, it seemed yet more wanted for Congress members. They moved in a higher sphere. By purchasing certificates with one hand, and making laws with the other, they could accumulate, as William Smith actually did, an enormous fortune. Their statute book has no prohibition against themselves, like that against persons in the treasury. The fatal act of August 4th, 1790, *making provision for the debt of the United States,* in the sequel, saddled the country with a burden of seventy-three millions of dollars. But if any member had bought up the whole budget for one per cent, no clause in the act forbade him to have done so, or inflicted the smallest penalty or censure whatever. Yet only eleven months before, Congress by a law, prohibited treasury officers to do what Congress themselves were actually doing.

If Dr. William Smith, and forty other members of the two houses, were entitled to trade in paper, they had no right of hindering any body else. Speculation was not to be hedged in for them. It was not like the feudal *Jus primi noctis*[5], or like the royal exercise of scratching, which James the Sixth declared to be too great a pleasure for a subject to enjoy. This first congress found for America what Jugurtha wanted for Rome, a merchant rich enough to buy her. Within

[4] Some of the certificates were bought, it is said, for ten pence per pound, with ten years of interest into the bargain.

[5] The privilege of the first night.

their twenty-three months of existence, that assembly gave to the constitution a blow from which it has almost no chance of recovering. . . .

In point of morality, the following is a summary of objections that occur to the national debt.

First. The funding law past through congress by the influence of a majority, who purchased certificates from the army at an under value; and who voted for the law, with the single view of enriching themselves. This manoeuvre almost entirely excluded the real holders of certificates from the benefit of the statute; and of consequence perverted the substantial ends of justice.

Second. Even if the law had operated only in favour of the original holders, still the arrangement was radically unjust; the privates receiving certificates only for one fifth part of the sums to which they were entitled.

Third. Although the rank and file had really been placed on a level with the officers, yet they had not a better claim to compensation than the myriads of other citizens, who lost their whole property by the extinction of congress paper money, and who are now actually taxed to pay the public debt. It is apprehended that, in a court of mere equity, these objections would be decisive against the *moral obligation* upon the public of paying this debt.

Fourth. As no man can transfer a title which he does not possess, every objection applicable to the original member of congress, enriched by the funding law, must apply to the assignees of any such creditor; they being, on the supposition of previous fraud, precisely in the situation of indorsees to a forged note; or the purchaser of a stolen horse. These remarks, as before explained, do not militate against the expediency of paying

off the public debt. They tend merely to explain the nature of the *moral obligation*. . . .

. . . the law for funding at twenty shillings per pound did not flow from solicitude of doing justice to real creditors. It was framed wholly and solely for the sake of glutting with the spoils of their country an host of repacious speculators. If the first congress had been anxious to act honestly, a straight road lay before them; and a resolution, or statute of ten lines, could have fulfilled every equitable end. They might have enjoined all first holders of certificates to lodge, within twelve months, a state of their claims at the treasury office, under a moderate penalty for neglect or delay. Of all future delays the necessity ought to have been decided, not by congress; for their subsequent proceedings on the statute of limitations discover, that they did not merit much confidence. A jury in the vicinage of the creditor would have been less expensive to him, and much more likely to do justice. The law should have been carefully promulgated in every county and township in the Union. The actual creditors might then have been paid to their full amount, extending probably to five or six millions of dollars. Congress might, at the same time, have appropriated an annual sum to agents for buying up the certificates held by assignees, at the cheapest rate for which they could be had, with an injunction not to exceed half a crown or perhaps three shillings per pound. Strong reasons have been given[6] why even the primitive holders were not entitled to such an eminent preference; yet, for the sake of internal tranquillity, it might have been expedient.

[6] Findley's Review of the Revenue System adopted by the first congress under the Federal Constitution, Chap. 2d.

The man from whose breast interest or faction has not obliterated every spark of justice, will acknowledge that this was the way in which the first congress should have extricated the Union from this unfathomable quagmire of public debt. No conjunction can be more completely monstrous than that of a legislator engrafted on a paper-jobber, ascending the chair of congress, and voting that he himself shall receive for a certificate ten or twelve times the value which it originally cost him.

Alexander Hamilton tries to escape from his quota of reproach by confessing something, that, if possible, is yet a viler crime. Not one of the congressional partners in this job wishes to hear a word about it.

The departure of Thomas Paine for Europe, previous to the production of the plan, inflicted a probable loss on the United States. A few seasonable pages from his celebrated and victorious pen might have scared into non-entity this hideous and gigantic spectre of gambling.

Mr. Findley affirms that Hamilton and his party never wanted to redeem the public debt, although this could in a great measure have been done by the sale of the Western lands. "Flint and Parker had agreed to purchase three millions of acres. To the second session of the New Congress, Scriba made proposals for four or five millions. And Hannibal William Dobbyne proposed to take more than all the others, and to settle it with people from Ireland. These proposals were referred to the secretary of the treasury, while he was privately preparing the funding system: but *he never reported on them*."[7] Such allegations were so notorious that they could not have been invented without instant detection.

They have not been denied. The obvious conclusion is that inferred by Mr. Findley. The federal party did not want to rid the United States of the debt. "If the proposals of Messrs. Parker, Dobbyne, and others, which were offered before the funding system was originated, had been accepted, it is a moderate computation to suppose that fifteen millions of dollars would have been redeemed."[8] By various means which Mr. Findley explains at considerable length, only six millions of dollars would have remained of the domestic debt, "to be funded or discharged by the general government, besides a small arrearage of interest."[9] Thus, even upon the plan of discharging the whole rubbish of speculation at twenty shillings per pound, and that would have been a deed of the wildest profusion, still the burden might have been reduced to the very small matter of six millions of dollars.

Mr. Hamilton does not disown his having neglected these glorious opportunities of extinguishing this oppressive load. An "objection on which the secretary of the treasury lays great stress, is, that to attempt purchasing in the public debt in an unfunded state, would be *highly dishonourable to government*."[10] That government possessed not an immense share of honour to lose. The Old Congress broke for two hundred millions of pasteboard dollars. A few remnants of this trash, which had evaded the tobacco pipe or the necessary, have since been funded at one hundred for one.[11] In other words, the new government engaged to give two pence and two-fifths per pound for the paper of the old congress, while

7 Ibid. Letter 1.

8 Ibid.

9 Ibid.

10 Findley, letter 1.

11 Gallatin, p. 89.

they were funding that of an army of artificial creditors, at twenty shillings.

He must be blind indeed who does not perceive the cloven foot of speculation sticking through Mr. Hamilton's pretence about *honour*. It might, at first sight, have been supposed that the purchasers of certificates would be very glad to get twenty shillings per pound in Western lands. Accordingly, Mr. Findley says that they were so. But Mr. Hamilton and his confidents had further views. By arrangements that have since taken place, they foresaw that the debt, if funded, might become a ladder for mounting up, not only to a national bank, but likewise to the administration of the country. Accordingly, during the first and second congress, they governed with absolute sway. The third congress made a vigorous stand, but were overpowered by the odium of the Western riots, and the interference of Jay's embassy. The senate of the third congress behaved with spirit. Mr. Madison's first resolution, and that of Mr. Clarke respecting British intercourse, were rejected only by the valuable and casting vote of Mr. Adams. But in the fourth congress the senate fell off. The representatives remained firm through the first session, till they were overborne by the clamour for passing Jay's treaty. To the fifth congress, Virginia has unfortunately sent three aristocratical representatives; and this is one of the chief reasons why the treasury has at present a majority of representatives, which is narrow, to be sure, but remarkably violent. The whole offices in the gift of the executive are held by that party, and their followers. In return they stretch every prerogative of the president as far as they possibly can.

It was perfectly understood, at the time when Hamilton made the above declaration, that he had motives very different from a respect for congressional *honour*, in wanting to fund the public debt. When the plan had been matured in his closet, "that closet was not so impervious, as to prevent the *favorite order* of speculators from knowing the principles of the system, before it saw the light, and improving that knowledge to their own advantage. — Specie was sent from New York in thirty thousand dollar cargoes, and the southern people, being unavoidably ignorant of the ministerial plan, were swindled out of their claims for a trifle."[12] Of one citizen of Philadelphia, it is here stated, on good information, that he dispatched a courier to North Carolina with six hundred hard dollars. He bought up a large quantity of certificates, with about ten years of interest due upon them. He is said to have netted by this manoeuvre about twenty-two thousand dollars. At ten pence per pound, six hundred dollars expand into fourteen thousand four hundred. In such cases, the blame falls not on private speculators, but on congress. Immense sums must also have been gained by foreigners, such as the house, above noticed, at New York, which held certificates for two millions of dollars. All these private speculations were of necessity countenanced, and funded at full value, for the sake of cloaking that part of the spoil acquired by members of the first congress. The profits arising to private citizens at home, and to foreigners abroad, were very much greater than those of our legislators themselves. An affair of probably thirty-five millions of dollars was too immense to be grasped by a junto of fifty or sixty individuals.

On January 1st, 1790, the whole domestic debt came to forty millions, two hundred and fifty-six thousand dollars.[13] Put

[12] Findley, Letter 2d.

[13] Gallatin, p. 96.

the case that original creditors held four millions, foreigners and private persons, twenty-four millions, and sixty legislators twelve millions, or two hundred thousand dollars per man. By this estimate, when Roger Sherman, or Dr. William Smith cleared *one* dollar, the primitive holders lost *three*. It is firmly believed and loudly asserted, by at least one half of the citizens of America, that the funding system was devised, not for the sake of paying the real creditors, but of wronging them. Hamilton planned. Congress voted. The president approved.

THE PEOPLE DEFEND HAMILTON'S DEBT PLAN

FISHER AMES: A LETTER TO GEORGE RICHARDS MINOT

Philadelphia, November 30, 1791. DEAR SIR, I am solicitous to keep alive the remembrance of me with my friends. Congress is so little minded in the transaction of the business of this session, that I must not confide in my drawing their attention, as a spoke in the political wheel. Therefore, I will make continual claim to your notice, whenever I begin to apprehend being forgotten, to such a degree as to overcome my lazy habits, and the difficulty arising from the dearth of matter.

The spirit of debate bears no proportion to the objects of debate. It may be a question with moral observers, which most inflames the zeal of members, the magnitude of the consequences which a measure will produce, or the sensibility to the contradiction of their opinions. I decide nothing on this delicate subject. But in fact several debates have arisen, like thundergusts in a pleasant day, when no Mr. Weatherwise would have guessed it. The ratio of representation seemed to me, beforehand, as pacific a question as

any public assembly ever slumbered over. But though the difference of opinion was narrowed within the limits of one to thirty or thirty-four thousand, yet eloquence, so long weary of rest, seemed to rejoice in the opportunity of stretching its limbs. We heard, and no doubt, if you had patience, you have read, about republicanism, and aristocracy, and corruption, and the sense of the people, and the amendments, and indeed so much good stuff, that I almost wonder it did not hold out longer. We have disputed about a mode of trying the disputed election of Generals Wayne and Jackson. To be serious, my friend, the great objects of the session are yet untouched; but the House, especially the new members, have been very often engaged in the *petite guerre*.

Instead of facts, I will notice to you, that the remark so often made on the difference of opinion between the members from the two ends of the continent, appears to me not only true, but founded on causes which are equally unpleasant and lasting. To the northward, we see

Reprinted in *Works of Fisher Ames*, Seth Ames, ed. (2 vols., Boston: Little, Brown and Company, 1854), I, 102–106.

how necessary it is to defend property by steady laws. Shays confirmed our habits and opinions. The men of sense and property, even a little above the multitude, wish to keep the government in force enough to govern. We have trade, money, credit, and industry, which is at once cause and effect of the others.

At the southward, a few gentlemen govern; the law is their coat of mail; it keeps off the weapons of the foreigners, their creditors, and at the same time it governs the multitude, secures negroes, &c., which is of double use to them. It is both government and anarchy, and in each case is better than any possible change, especially in favor of an exterior (or federal) government of any strength; for that would be losing the property, the usufruct of a government, by the State, which is light to bear and convenient to manage. Therefore, and for other causes, the men of weight in the four southern States (Charleston city excepted) were more generally *antis*, and are now far more turbulent than they are with us. Many were federal among them at first, because they needed some remedy to evils which they saw and felt, but mistook, in their view of it, the remedy. A debt-compelling government is no remedy to men who have lands and negroes, and debts and luxury, but neither trade nor credit, nor cash, nor the habits of industry, or of submission to a rigid execution of law. My friend, you will agree with me, that, ultimately, the same system of strict law, which has done wonders for us, would promote their advantage. But that relief is speculative and remote. Enormous debts required something better and speedier. I am told that, to this day, no British debt is recovered in North Carolina. This, however, I can scarcely credit, though I had strong evidence of its truth. You will

agree that our immediate wants were different — we to enforce, they to relax, law. The effects of these causes on opinions have been considerable, as you will suppose. Various circumstances, some merely casual, have multiplied them.

Patrick Henry, and some others of eminent talents, and influence, have continued *antis*, and have assiduously nursed the embryos of faction, which the adoption of the Constitution did not destroy. It soon gave popularity to the *antis* with a grumbling multitude. It made two parties.

Most of the measures of Congress have been opposed by the southern members. I speak not merely of their members, but their gentlemen, &c., at home. As men, they are mostly enlightened, clever fellows. I speak of the tendency of things, upon their politics, not their morals. This has sharpened discontent at home. The funding system, they say, is in favor of the moneyed interest — oppressive to the land; that is, favorable to us, hard on them. They pay tribute, they say, and the middle and eastern people, holders of seven eighths of the debt, receive it. And here is the burden of the song, almost all the little that they had and which cost them twenty shillings for supplies or services, has been bought up, at a low rate, and now they pay more tax towards the interest than they received for the paper. This *tribute*, they say, is aggravating, for all the reasons before given; they add, had the State debts not been assumed they would have wiped it off among themselves very speedily and easily. Being assumed, it has become a great debt; and now an excise, that abhorrence of free States, must pay it. This they have never adopted in their States. The States of Virginia, North Carolina, and Georgia are large territories. Being strong, and expecting by increase to be stronger, the government of Congress over them seems mortifying to their State pride. The pride of the strong is not soothed by yielding to a stronger. How much there is, and how much more can be made of all these themes of grief and anger, by men who are inclined and qualified to make the most of them, need not be pointed out to a man, who has seen so much, and written so well, upon the principles which disturb and endanger government.

I confess I have recited these causes rather more at length than I had intended. But you are an observer, and I hope will be a writer of our history. The picture I have drawn, though just, is not noticed. Public happiness is in our power as a nation. Tranquillity has smoothed the surface. But (what I have said of southern parties is so true that I may affirm) faction glows within like a coalpit. The President lives — is a southern man, is venerated as a demi-god, he is chosen by unanimous vote, &c., &c. Change the key and . . . You can fill up the blank. But, while he lives, a steady prudent system by Congress may guard against the danger. Peace will enrich our southern friends. Good laws will establish more industry and economy. The peculiar causes of discontent will have lost their force with time. Yet, circumstanced as they are, I think other subjects of uneasiness will be found. For it is impossible to administer the government according to their ideas. We must have a revenue; of course an excise. The debt must be kept sacred; the rights of property must be held inviolate. We must, to be safe, have some regular force, and an efficient militia. All these, except the last, and that, except in a form not worth having, are obnoxious to them. I have not noticed what they call their republicanism, because having observed what their situation is, you will see what their theory must be, in seeing what it is drawn from. I have not exhausted, but I quit this part of the subject. In fine, those three States are circumstanced not unlike our State in 1786.

I think these deductions flow from the premises: That the strength as well as hopes of the union reside with the middle and eastern States. That our good men must watch and pray on all proper occasions for the preservation of federal measures, and principles. That so far from being in a condition to swallow up the State governments, Congress cannot be presumed to possess too much force to preserve its constitutional authority, whenever the crisis, to which these discontents are hastening, shall have brought its power to the test. And, above all, that, in the supposed crisis, the State partisans, who seem to wish to clip the wings of the union, would be not the least zealous to support the union. For, zealous as they may be to extend the power of the General Court of Massachusetts, they would not wish to be controlled by that of Virginia. I will not tire you with more speculation; but I will confess my belief that if, now, a vote was to be taken, "Shall the Constitution be adopted," and the people of Virginia, and the other more southern States, (the city of Charleston excepted,) should answer instantly, according to their present feelings and opinions, it would be in the negative.

These are dangers which our Massachusetts parties probably do not know, and have not weighed, and I shall hope that if they should be brought to view them in as alarming forms as it is an even chance they will, we shall have there but one sentiment. We ought to have but one. My paper is out, so farewell.

Your affectionate friend, &c.

FISHER AMES

A COMMUNICATION TO THE *PENNSYLVANIA GAZETTE*
February 3, 1790

Messrs. Hall & Sellers,

I have observed, for some years back, a variety of publications, such as they have been, respecting alienated certificates, which the present holders have treated with that neglect they merited. I will, however, offer a few considerations on the subject.

The holders of such certificates are called speculators. And what then? Is not every member of the community a speculator? Is it not as just and as honorable to speculate in certificates, as in houses, land, articles of merchandize, &c. Nay, in many instances much more so: Especially, when the present holders had compassion on the original holders, and bought their certificates at the market price, and at a considerable risque, while those of toryish principles would not touch them; and I am mistaken, if it be not these that are now endeavouring to raise an outcry.

But the certificates have altered in value. Very true. And what species of property is it that has not undergone the same fate, gold itself not excepted. Did they not change value in the hands of the holders for the time being? Must not every holder of property, be it of what kind it may, abide by the change of its value? Have not houses and land fell one half in value within ten years? He that sells a house or land for five hundred pounds, for which he gave a thousand pounds but a few years ago, must he come on the person he bought it of, or does any one dream that he ought to petition Congress?

If the holders of alienated certificates are to be stripped of their property, it must be on the footing of equity, or justice, or the leveling principle. The latter of these would, I imagine, suit a great many among us; and something of it, I fear, is in fact at bottom, if those writers alluded to above would but speak out plainly.

As for the claims of the holders of the certificates in question on the footing of the law, we all know it cannot be disputed. Should it be pretended that there is or may be a claim against them in equity, where will it end? Is there not the same claim against those, who have purchased houses or land, &c? Did not he, who gave six shillings in the pound for a certificate, did he not give a more valuable consideration for it than many of the original holders? What shall we say of many of the staff-department? What of depreciation certificates? Did not the whole community suffer by depreciation? What shall we say of commutation certificates, which amount to millions of dollars. Was there any service rendered for them? I would not be understood to mean that any of those should be robbed of their just property. Far be it from me. I have no idea of sacrificing public faith at that rate, nor at any rate. But I will not hesitate to say, that the present holders of alienated certificates have as good, and, generally speaking, a much better claim than the above, whether you take it on the footing of justice or equity.

A CUSTOMER

A COMMUNICATION TO THE *GAZETTE OF THE UNITED STATES*
February 18, 1792

Mr. Fenno,

I am a plain farmer; and as the winter evenings are long, I love to get the city papers and to con over the affairs of the nation. My own affairs go very well; wheat has sold very well since the new government began, the crops have been good, and I find since the debt has made such a fuss I get the ready cash better than ever, for cash is grown plenty. Thus I am quite at leisure to mind what does not more concern me than another man. I have a family, however, and I look forward to futurity as I ought. No body will wonder then that I am a deep politician. I have read the city papers till the cold sweat ran down my face — I never sweated more at the plow. I read about the danger that our republican principles are exposed to, and how monied men are growing up to the size of Goliath, and how Congress is all wrong, and how we are too rich now to be virtuous and free, tho t'other day we were too poor to pay for a government, and then the charge of it would take our bread away, and our children would cry for a crust. I love my family as well as a bird loves her nest, and my children as well as she loves her young. I had rather secure to them a good education and a free government, than to learn them to dance and leave behind me a great estate. I have been led into an hundred scrapes by thinking too well of my own opinion, and so says I, I will see how the wind is with my neighbors, for we live mighty well together. A dozen of us got together on new year's evening, and then we talked all these matters over.

If we had drinked small beer, it would be a short story to tell you all that passed, but as small beer would not go down we were all very talkative — we did not drink to excess however. Instead of telling you all that was said, it will be sufficient to tell you what was finally agreed to.

The funding system was at first condemned as very improper, and anti-republican — but after mature enquiry it was allowed that it was a very good thing. What does that promise, said we, more than to pay our just debts — Debts contracted to make the lands we live on our own, and to remove a stranger and intruder from them. Tho we pay at 20s. in the pound, as some complain, we had the value at that time when the debt was contracted, and now we have the benefit more than twenty fold, having beaten our enemies, and being set down to enjoy peace and security under a free government. If then we owe the debt, what harm to promise to pay it. The funding system acknowledges the debt, and engages to pay the interest quarterly. Something was to be done with the debt — Congress must either pay the principal of the debt at once, or pay the interest yearly by annual grants, or fund it as they have done, or take the spunge and rub it out. When we blame Congress for the way they have pursued, it is but fair to see what other ways lay open for them. We should not have thanked Congress to call for a direct tax to pay off the debt at once. We had not the money. Such a great demand would have crushed us, and it is out of the question. Had Congress forborne to fund the debt, it would have been a better speculating scheme than it is now. The more uncertain from year to year, the better for the speculators. They would have speculated on the chance that the interest would not be voted for at the year's end. Who would have been the gainers by this uncertainty. Not the farmers. The money would have been drawn to the seaports, where this scheme of yearly grants for the interest would have opened the most profitable market for money. Therefore few would have engaged in the improvements or purchase of lands. And the debt itself, tho always employing money, would not have taken the place of money as it has done of late. Another very bad consequence has been told us, that foreigners would have got the certificates for a trifle. It is true they have bought them since the debt was funded, but we have got into the country 24s. or 25s. for every 20s. We receive more than we give, and it is not easy to see how the country can be made poor by making good bargains. Why then should we not fund the debt at once. We mean to pay it — where was the harm of saying so. The last method of disposing of the debt was to blot it out. Some people think that would be throwing off a weight they are tired of carrying on their backs. Now, I teach my children the ten commandments. I endeavor to bring them up to be honest men — and I should be miserable if I foresaw that they would be brought to shame for their misdeeds. I should truly be afraid of their turning out rogues in spite of my care, if Congress had agreed to spunge out the debt. Government, by shewing what advantage is to be got by dishonesty, would do a great deal towards spoiling all the youth in the land. Therefore, if the devil tempted Congress to jockey the public creditors, I am glad for my children's sake they did not yield to him.

Some have found fault because the whole debt cannot be redeemed at pleasure. Where is the harm of that, pray? We have taken a stout slice from the creditors on that account; and have we parted with any very valuable rights? Have we not reserved the right to redeem as much of the debt as we have money to pay off. And what a rout is kept up in the news-papers, because we have parted with the right to do what we cannot do. And yet we have been well paid for parting with the right by the funding system, i.e. by the 3 per cents and deferred debt.

This is alleged to be dangerous to a republican people. There may be a snake in the grass, but I cannot see how a people expose themselves by acting according to good conscience. We owe the debt, and we ought to pay it as soon as we can. I cannot for my life see what there is anti-republican in pursuing the plain old path of common honesty.

As to the fiddle-faddle story of the great nabobs becoming lords, I feel quite at my ease. They must leave off getting children — otherwise half a dozen or half a score young fellows in each family, will be found to have a greater inheritance in folly and luxury than in 6 per cents. And what care we, the lords of the soil, for the six per cent gentry. Their wealth gives them no power over us — and as to their number and influence, they will affect the price of pheasants and venison more than the votes of the yeomanry. The country is in the hands of the landed interest — which outweighs as much as it outnumbers the monied interest. The latter has ever been as a drop in the bucket: and though it has increased of late very unexpectedly, the landed interest has not increased less — and it is going on with a speed and to an extent that mocks the silly apprehensions of the monied interest eating it up. Look round and see how the frontier circle widens — see how the interior part improves — see how arts and manufactures multiply — A man who stands on a wharf, sees none of this wonderful growth of the landed interest — he sees the growth of trade, which indeed flows from the growth of the country produce — he sees the merchants and rich people scattering handfulls of money for luxuries, and he is ready to cry out that the newspapers are in the right to sound the alarm for liberty; and so he snatches his pen and ink to tell us how we are made beggars by growing rich, and all slaves by honest and equal laws. But the landed interest governs every country — and as in this men live on their own farms, and are not tenants, nothing is more certain than that the people may govern if they will. Liberty is not exposed to any new danger by the new monied interest, as the public creditors are termed by the angry newspaper writers. On the contrary, it is plain that these men will lose more than other citizens by the destruction of the common liberty — for their property is made to depend wholly on the laws — their policy is to keep all quiet, not to change the government, as many insinuate. It would be a queer blunder for a man of six per cent to join in a plot against a free government, which pays him his income. Liberty, therefore, has gained new friends rather than foes by the funding system — whose livings are made to depend on their support of the present free and equal system of laws.

On the whole, no country ever gained more credit, wealth and power, in three year's time, than this has done since the new government began. If the newspapers are full of charges against the government which has chiefly produced this wonderful change — at the very moment when the change is fresh in our minds, and if they are capable of souring the people against it in the prosperous outset — What will happen when mistakes or disasters, incident to all governments, shall have destroyed its popularity? It will be torn limb from limb, unless the body of the people, who form its solid support, shall be willing to protect it against its artful and implacable enemies. Of all its friends, the farmers should be the firmest; for Congress lays no land taxes, and yet things go on very well — too well, say the newspapers. And whether it encourages manufacturers to eat the provisions at home, or navigation to seek a market abroad, we are sure of the benefit. Oppression will make a wise man mad. If only talking about oppression when there is none, will make a man mad, I will say he is not a wise man.

A FARMER

AN EDITORIAL IN THE *GAZETTE OF THE UNITED STATES*
September 5, 1792

A writer in one of the Eastern papers, says — "It is with singular pleasure I observe the thriving state of agriculture, commerce, and arts in every part of the country I have visited. At no former period of the last twenty-five years, have people so generally enjoyed the blessings of peace, plenty and satisfaction. It is a remark of farmers in the interior country, that people were never before so industrious, and never acquired property so fast as at the present time. This industry is, through the northern states, rewarded with the most plentiful crops ever known. Three years ago industry languished, and multitudes of people were wandering about the country in quest of employment. Day laborers were about the streets of our large towns in herds. But times are changed. It is now almost impossible to procure laborers at any price. In the town and country there is more employment than men — the mechanic's undertaking retarded, and the farmers crops waiting in the field for want of laborers. Even emigration to the western lands is checked by this favorable state of business.

"Let the reader pause a moment and enquire what is the cause of this new and unexpected change of affairs. To what physical, moral or political energy shall this flourishing state of things be ascribed? There is but one answer to these enquiries: *Public credit is restored and established.* The general government, by uniting, and calling into action, the pecuniary resources of the states, has created a new capital stock of several millions of dollars, which, with that before existing, is directed into every branch of business, giving life and vigor to industry in its infinitely diversified operations. The enemies of the general government, the funding act and the National Bank, may bellow *tyranny, aristocracy,* and *Speculators* through the Union, and repeat the clamorous din as long as they please; but the actual state of agriculture and commerce, the peace, the contentment and satisfaction of the great mass of people, give the lie to their assertions, and stamp on them in capitals,

Vox et praeterea nihil. It is surprising this pouting whining herd of disappointed wrong-heads will not be silent and retire with shame from public notice, when they see all their visionary predictions falsified, and instead of their expected calamities, they see the public mind at ease, and all parts of the community congratulating each other on the full enjoyment of the blessings of peace, liberty, safety and general prosperity. One would think that baffled ambition itself would retire from assailing our ears and annoying our happiness; after having for two years murmured out its puny whinings in vain. But why should government be exempted from the vexations of harboring foes in its bosom? There was a Judas among the disciples of Jesus, and the joys of paradise were interrupted by the restless ambition of a Satan. How then can the most perfect system of human government satisfy all the wants and wishes of its subjects?

"And little *less* than angels, would be *more.*"

HAMILTON IN HIS OWN DEFENSE

VINDICATION OF THE FUNDING SYSTEM

Number One

1791 (?)

It was to have been foreseen, that though the virtuous part of those who were opposed to the present Constitution of the United States, while in deliberation before the people, would yield to the evidence which experience would afford

of its usefulness and safety, there were opponents of a certain character, who, as happens in all great political questions, would always remain incurably hostile to it; that in the course of its administration its greatest merits would be in the eyes of such men its greatest blemishes, its most brilliant successes to them occasions

Both this and the following selection are reprinted in *The Works of Alexander Hamilton*, Henry Cabot Lodge, ed. (New York: G. P. Putnam's Sons, 1885), II, 285–290, 237–238, 241–242, 253–254, 274–278.

of bitter chagrin and envious detraction, its slightest mismanagements subjects of malignant exaggeration, its most trivial misfortunes the welcome topics of virulent accusation and insidious misrepresentation.

With some men the hardest thing to forgive is the demonstration of their errors, the manifestation that they are not infallible. Mortified vanity is one of the most corroding emotions of the human mind; one of the most unextinguishable sources of animosity and hatred.

It was equally to have been foreseen, that personal disappointments would be likely to alienate from the government some individuals who had at first advocated its adoption, perhaps from motives not the most patriotic or commendable; that personal rivalships and competitions would throw others into an opposition to its measures, without much regard to their intrinsic merits or demerits; and that a third class would embrace the path of opposition as the supposed road to popularity and preferment, raising upon every colorable pretext the cry of danger to liberty, and endeavoring to disseminate among the people false terrors and ill-grounded alarms.

Phenomena like these have deformed the political horizon, and testified the depravity of mankind, in all countries and at all times.

It was likewise to have been expected that among the well-meaning friends of the government, there would be a part, competent to the proper management of the affairs of the Union, who, sensible from experience of the insufficiency of the former system, gave their assent to the substitute offered to their choice, rather from general impressions of the necessity of a change, than from an accurate view of the necessary compass of the authorities which ought to constitute it.

When they came to witness the exercise of those authorities upon a scale more comprehensive than they had contemplated, and to hear the incendiary comments of those who will ever be on the watch for pretexts to brand the proceedings of the government with imputations of usurpation and tyranny, and the factious and indiscreet clamors of those who, in and out of the Legislature, with too much levity, torture the Constitution into objections to measures which they deem inexpedient; it was to have been expected, I say, that some such men might be carried away by transient anxieties and apprehensions, and might for a moment add weight to an opposition which could not fail to grow out of other causes, and the real objects of which they would abhor.

There is yet another class of men, who, in all the stages of our republican system, either from desperate circumstances, or irregular ambition, or a mixture of both, will labor incessantly to keep the government in a troubled and unsettled state, to sow disquietudes in the minds of the people, and to promote confusion and change. Every republic at all times has its Catilines and its Caesars.

Men of this stamp, while in their hearts they scoff at the principles of liberty, while in their real characters they are arbitrary, persecuting, and intolerant, are in all their harangues and professions the most zealous; nay, if they are to be believed, the only friends of liberty. Mercenary and corrupt themselves, they are continually making a parade of their purity and disinterestedness, and heaping upon others charges of peculation and corruption. Extravagant and dissipated in their own affairs, they are always prating about public economy, and railing at the government for its pretended profusion. Conscious that as long as the confidence of the people shall be maintained in their tried and faithful servants, in men of real integrity and patriotism, their ambitious projects can never succeed, they leave no artifice unessayed, they spare no pains to destroy that confidence, and blacken the characters that stand in their way.

Convinced that as long as order and system in the public affairs can be maintained, their schemes can never be realized, they are constantly representing the means of that order and system as chains forged for the people. Themselves the only plotters and conspirators, they are for ever spreading tales of plots and conspiracies; always talking of the republican cause, and meaning nothing but the cause of themselves and their party; virtue and liberty constantly on their lips, fraud, usurpation, and tyranny in their hearts.

There is yet another class of opponents to the government and its administration, who are of too much consequence not to be mentioned: a sect of political doctors; a kind of POPES in government; standards of political orthodoxy, who brand with heresy all opinions but their own; men of sublimated imaginations and weak judgments; pretenders to profound knowledge, yet ignorant of the most useful of all sciences — the science of human nature; men who dignify themselves with the appellation of philosophers, yet are destitute of the first elements of true philosophy; lovers of paradoxes; men who maintain expressly that religion is not necessary to society, and very nearly that government itself is a nuisance; that priests and clergymen of all descriptions are worse than useless. Such men, the ridicule of any cause that they espouse, and the best witnesses to the goodness of that which they oppose, have no small share in the clamors which are raised, and in the dissatisfactions which are excited.

While the real object of these clamors, with the persons most active in propagating them, is opposition to the administration of it; while they are straining every nerve to render it odious, they are profuse in their professions of attachment to it. To oppose avowedly the *work of the people* would be too barefaced. It would not accord with that system of treacherous flattery, which is the usual engine of these pretended "friends," but real betrayers, of the people.

Circumstances require that the mode of attack be changed. The government is to be good, if not excellent, but its administration is to be execrable — detestable — a mere sink of corruption; a deep-laid plan to overturn the republican system of the country.

Suspicions of the most flagitious prostitution and corruption in office, of improper connections with brokers and speculators to fleece the community, of the horrid depravity of promoting wars, and the shedding of human blood, for the sake of sharing collusively the emoluments of lucrative contracts, suspicions like these are, if possible, to be thrown upon men, the whole tenor of whose lives gives the lie to them; who, before they came into office, were never either *land*-jobbers, or stock-jobbers, or jobbers of any other kind; who can appeal to their fellow-citizens of every other party and description to attest that their reputations for probity are unsullied, that their conduct in all pecuniary concerns has been nicely correct and even exemplarily disinterested; who, it is notorious, have sacrificed and are sacrificing the interests of their families to their public zeal; who, whenever the necessity of resisting the machinations of the enemies of the public quiet will permit them to retire, will retire poorer than they came into office, and will have to resume under numerous disadvantages the pursuits which they before followed under every advantage. Shame, where is thy blush? — if detraction so malignant as this can affront the public ear. Integrity, where is thy shield? where thy reward? — if the poisonous breath of an unprincipled cabal can pollute thy good name which thou incessantly toiled to deserve.

People of America, can ye be deceived by arts like these? Will ye suffer yourselves to be cheated out of your confidence in men who deserve it most? Will ye be the dupes of hypocritical pretenders?

OBJECTIONS AND ANSWERS RESPECTING THE ADMINISTRATION OF THE GOVERNMENT: A REPLY TO AN INQUIRY WHICH HAMILTON RECEIVED FROM GEORGE WASHINGTON

Philadelphia, *August 18, 1792.*

SIR: I am happy to be able, at length, to send you answers to the objections which were communicated in your letter of the 29th of July.

They have unavoidably been drawn in haste, too much so, to do perfect justice to the subject, and have been copied just as they flowed from my heart and pen, without revision or correction. You will observe that here and there some severity appears. I have not fortitude enough always to hear with calmness calumnies which necessarily include me, as a principal agent in the measures censured, of the falsehood of which I have the most unqualified consciousness. I trust I shall always be able to bear, as I ought, imputations of errors of judgment; but I acknowledge that I cannot be entirely patient under charges which impeach the integrity of my public motives or conduct. I feel that I merit them *in no degree;* and expressions of indignation sometimes escape me, in spite of every effort to suppress them. I rely on your goodness for the proper allowances.

With high respect and the most affectionate attachment, I have the honor to be, sir, etc.

OBJECTION: — The public debt is greater than we can possibly pay before other causes of adding to it will occur . . .

ANSWER: — The public debt was produced by the late war. It is not the fault of the present government that it exists, unless it can be proved that public morality and policy do not require of a government an honest provision for its debts. Whether it is greater than can be paid before new causes of adding to it will occur, is a problem incapable of being solved, but by experience; and this would be the case if it were not one fourth as much as it is. If the policy of the country be prudent, cautious, and neutral towards foreign nations, there is a rational probability that war may be avoided long enough to wipe off the debt. The Dutch, in a situation not near so favorable for it as that of the United States, have enjoyed intervals of peace longer than with proper exertions would suffice for the purpose. The debt of the United States, compared with its present and growing abilities, is really a very light one. It is little more than 15,000,000 of pounds sterling — about the annual expenditure of Great Britain.

But whether the public debt shall be extinguished or not, within a moderate period, depends on the temper of the people. If they are rendered dissatisfied by misrepresentations of the measures of the government, the government will be deprived of an efficient command of the resources of the community toward extinguishing the debt. And thus those who clamor are likely to be the principal causes of protracting the existence of the debt. . . .

How the thing [assumption] may work upon the whole cannot be pronounced without a knowledge of the situation of the account of each State; but all circumstances that are known render it probable that the ultimate effect will be favorable to justice between the States, and that there will be inconsiderable balances either on one side or on the other.

It was observed, that perhaps the true reproach of the system which has been adopted is, that it has artificially decreased the debt. This is explained thus:

In the case of the debt of the United States, interest upon two thirds of the principal only, at six per cent, is immediately paid; interest upon the remaining third was deferred for ten years, and only three per cent has been allowed upon the arrears of interest, making one third of the whole debt.

In the case of the separate debts of the States, interest upon four ninths only of the entire sum is immediately paid; interest upon two ninths was deferred for ten years, and only three per cent allowed on three ninths.

The market rate of interest, at the time of adopting the funding system, was six per cent. Computing, according to this rate of interest, the then present value of one hundred dollars of debt, upon an average, principal and interest, was about seventy-three dollars.

At the present *actual* value, in the market, of one hundred dollars, as the several kinds of stock are sold, is no more than eighty-three dollars and sixty-one cents. This computation is not made on equal sums of the several kinds of stock, according to which the average value of one hundred dollars would be only seventy-eight dollars and seventy-five cents; but it is made on the proportions which constitute the mass of the debt.

At seventy-three to one hundred, the diminution on 60,000,000 is 16,200,000 dollars; at eighty-three dollars and sixty-one cents to one hundred, it is 9,834,000 dollars.

But as the United States, having a right to redeem in certain proportions, need never give more than par for the six per cents, the diminution to them, as purchasers at the present market prices, is 12,168,000 dollars.

If it be said that the United States are engaged to pay the whole sum, at the nominal value, the answer is, that they are always at liberty, if they have the means, to purchase at the market prices; and in all those purchases they gain the difference between the nominal sums and the lesser market rates.

If the whole debt had been provided for at six per cent, the market rate of interest when the funding system passed, the market value throughout would undoubtedly have been one hundred for one hundred. The debt may then rather be said to have been artificially decreased by the nature of the provision.

The conclusion from the whole is that, assuming it as a principle that the public debts of the different descriptions were honestly to be provided for and paid, it is the reverse of true that there has been an artificial increase of them. To argue on a different principle, is to presuppose dishonesty, and make it an objection to doing right. . . .

In reality, on the principles of the funding system, the United States reduced the interest on their whole debt, upon an average, to about four and a half per cent, nearly the lowest rate they have any chance to borrow at, and lower than they could possibly have borrowed at in an attempt to reduce the interest on the whole capital by borrowing and paying, probably by one per cent. A demand for large loans, by forcing the market, would unavoidably have raised their price upon the borrower. The above average of four and a half per cent is found by calculation, computing the then present value of the deferred stock at the time of passing the funding acts, and of course three per cent on the three per cent stock.

The funding system, then, secured in the very outset the *precise advantage* which it is alleged would have accrued from having the whole debt redeemable at pleasure. But this is not all. It did more. It left the government still in a condition to enjoy upon five ninths of the entire debt the advantage of extinguishing it, by loans at a low rate of interest, if they are obtainable. The three per cents, which are one third of the whole, may always be purchased in the market below par, till the market rate of interest falls to three per cent. The deferred will be purchasable below par, till near the period of the actual payment of interest. And this further advantage will result: in all those purchases the public will enjoy, not only the advantage of a reduction of interest on the sums borrowed, but the additional advantage of purchasing the debt under par, that is, for less than twenty shillings in the pound.

If it be said that the like advantage might have been enjoyed under another system, the assertion would be without foundation. Unless some equivalent had been given for the reduction of interest in the irredeemable quality annexed to the debt, nothing was left, consistently with the principles of public credit, but to provide for the whole debt at six per

cent. This evidently would have kept the whole at par, and no advantage could have been derived by purchases under the nominal value. The reduction of interest, by borrowing at a lower rate, is all that would have been practicable, and this advantage has been secured by the funding system in the very outset, and without any second process.

If no provision for the interest had been made, not only public credit would have been sacrificed, but by means of it the borrowing at a low rate of interest, or at any rate, would have been impracticable.

There is no reproach which has been thrown upon the funding system so unmerited as that which charges it with being a bad bargain for the public, or with a tendency to prolong the extinguishment of the debts. The bargain has, if any thing, been too good on the side of the public; and it is impossible for the debt to be in a more convenient form than it is for a rapid extinguishment. . . .

OBJECTION: — The owners of the debt are in the Southern, and the holders of it in the Northern, division.

ANSWER: — If this were literally true, it would be no argument for or against any thing. It would be still politically and morally right for the debtors to pay their creditors.

But it is in *no sense true*. The *owners* of the debt are the people of *every* State, South, Middle, and North. The holders are the individual creditors — citizens of the United Netherlands, Great Britain, France, and of these States, North, Middle, South. Though some men, who constantly substitute hypothesis to fact, imagination to evidence, assert and reassert that the inhabitants of the South contribute *more* than those of the North, yet there is no pretence that they contribute *all;* and even the assertion of greater contribution is unsupported by documents, facts, or, it may be added, probabilities. Though the inhabitants of the South manufacture less than those of the North, which is the great argument, yet it does not follow that they consume more of taxable articles. It is a solid answer to this, that *whites* live better, wear more and better clothes, and consume more luxuries, than blacks, who constitute so considerable a part of the population of the South; that the inhabitants of cities and towns, which abound so much more in the North than in the South, consume more of foreign articles than the inhabitants of the country; that it is a general rule, that communities consume and contribute in proportion to their active or circulating wealth, and that the Northern regions have more active or circulating wealth than the Southern.

If official documents are consulted, though, for obvious reasons, they are not decisive, they contradict rather than confirm the hypothesis of greater proportional contribution in the Southern division.

But, to make the allegation in the objection true, it is necessary not merely that the inhabitants of the South should contribute more, but that they should contribute *all.*

It must be confessed that a much larger proportion of the debt is owned by inhabitants of the States from Pennsylvania to New Hampshire, inclusively, than in the States south of Pennsylvania.

But as to the primitive debt of the United States, that was the case in its original concoction. This arose from two causes: first, from the war having more constantly been carried on in the Northern quarter, which led to obtaining more men and greater supplies in that quarter,

and credit having been for a considerable time the main instrument of the government, a consequent accumulation of debt in that quarter took place; secondly, from the greater ability of the Northern and Middle States to furnish men, money, and other supplies, and from the greater quantities of men, money, and other supplies which they did furnish. The loan-office debt, the army debt, the debt of the five great departments, was contracted in a much larger proportion in the Northern and Middle, than in the Southern, States.

It must be confessed, too, that by the attraction of a superior moneyed capital the disparity has increased, but it was great in the beginning.

As to the assumed debt, the proportion in the South was at the first somewhat larger than in the North, and it must be acknowledged that this has since, from the same superiority of moneyed capital in the North, ceased to be the case.

But if the Northern people who were originally greater creditors than the Southern, have become still more so as purchasers, is it any reason that an honorable provision should not be made for their debt? Or is the government to blame for having made it? Did the Northern people take their property by violence from the Southern, or did they purchase and pay for it?

It may be answered that they obtained considerable part of it by speculation, taking advantage of superior opportunities for information.

But admitting this to be true in all the latitude in which it is commonly stated, is a government to bend the general maxims of policy and to mould its measures according to the accidental course of private speculations? Is it to do this, or omit that, in cases of great national importance, because one set of individuals may gain, another lose, from unequal opportunities of information, from unequal degrees of resource, craft, confidence, or enterprise?

Moreover, there is much exaggeration in stating the manner of the alienation of the debt. The principal speculations in State debts, whatever may be pretended, certainly began after the promulgation of the plan for assuming by the report of the Secretary of the Treasury to the House of Representatives. The resources of individuals in this country are too limited to have admitted of much progress in purchases before the knowledge of that plan was diffused throughout the country. After that, purchasers and sellers were upon equal ground. If the purchasers speculated upon the sellers, in many instances the sellers speculated upon the purchasers. Each made his calculation of chances, and founded upon it an exchange of money for certificates. It has turned out generally that the buyer had the best of the bargain, but the seller got the value of his commodity according to his estimate of it, and probably in a great number of instances more. This shall be explained.

It happened that Mr. Madison and some other distinguished characters of the South started in opposition to the assumption. The high opinion entertained of them made it be taken for granted in that quarter that the opposition would be successful. The securities quickly rose, by means of purchases, beyond their former prices. It was imagined that they would soon return to their old station by a rejection of the proposition for assuming. And the certificateholders were eager to part with them at their current prices, calculating on a loss

to the purchasers from their future fall. This representation is not conjectural; it is founded on information from respectable and intelligent Southern characters, and may be ascertained by inquiry.

Hence it happened that the inhabitants of the Southern States sustained a considerable loss by the opposition to the assumption from Southern gentlemen, and their too great confidence in the efficacy of that opposition.

Further, a great part of the debt which has been purchased by Northern and Southern citizens has been at higher prices — in numerous instances beyond the true value. In the late delirium of speculation large sums were purchased at twenty-five per cent above par and upward.

The Southern people, upon the whole, have not parted with their property for nothing. They parted with it voluntarily, in most cases, upon fair terms, without surprise or deception — in many cases for more than its value. 'T is their own fault if the purchase money has not been beneficial to them; and the presumption is, it has been so in a material degree.

Let, then, any candid and upright mind, weighing all the circumstances, pronounce whether there be any real hardship in the inhabitants of the South being required to contribute their proportion to a provision for the debt as it now exists? whether, if at liberty, they could honestly dispute the doing of it? or whether they can, even in candor and good faith, complain of being obliged to do it?

If they can, it is time to unlearn all the ancient notions of justice and morality, and to adopt a new system of ethics. . . .

Henry Cabot Lodge: THE RESULTS OF THE FINANCIAL POLICY

THE publication of the first report on the public credit was awaited with intense eagerness. When it came, there was, of course, much excitement and a general rise in the securities of the bankrupt Confederation. Eager speculators hurried over the country to buy up the debt, and the secretary of the treasury already began to be regarded as one who could make the fortune not only of the government but of individuals. Congress having decided that they would not listen to the perilous oratory of Hamilton, but confine him to writing, took up the report. As to the payment of the foreign debt, all were agreed, and that portion was adopted without discussion; but on the payment of the domestic debt a fierce conflict arose. The root of this opposition was in the old repudiating, disintegrating spirit of the Confederation which still survived, and which found even plainer expression in resistance to Hamilton's proposition to pay the arrears of interest in the same way as all other indebtedness. No one, however, was ready to take this stand against the domestic debt and advocate its absolute repudiation; perhaps, indeed, no one really desired such a proceeding in its fullest extent, although the old demoralization was really at the bottom of the hostility. The opposition sought to thwart the secretary and maim his plans, on grounds in appearance more reasonable and certainly more likely to arouse popular sympathy. They found their opening in the speculation which had begun with the adoption of the Constitution, and which reached a fever heat on the publication of the secretary's report, when the certificates of debt had bounded up to high prices at a single jump. The obvious cry was against the greedy and successful speculator in possession of the certificates, which he had obtained for a song from the original holders. The "original holder" now figured as a patriot cruelly wronged, and in many instances he was a soldier, which gave an additional point to the lamentations in his behalf, raised generally by men who, under the old Confederation, which still held their affections, had flouted with utter indifference all claims, both of soldier and patriotic leader.

But this inconsistency did not affect the value of the argument as a political cry. And there was, too, some ground for it in many cases of undoubted hardship. Hamilton and his friends freely admitted the force of this objection, but the secretary argued that the great object was to restore the credit and good name of the United States, to do what was just in the majority of instances and to the greatest number, and he urged, in conclusion, that any other course was impracticable. His reasoning could not be answered, but it did not quell the conflict. One proposition was, in cases where the certificate was in the hands of a purchaser, to pay him only what he had himself paid the original holder. The vio-

From *Alexander Hamilton* by Henry Cabot Lodge, pp. 115–133. Houghton Mifflin and Company, 1898. Reprinted by permission.

lation of contracts thus involved was the
fatal objection of Hamilton; but this plan
carried with it, moreover, a very deep
mark of the lurking desire to get out of
debt by partial repudiation. To the surprise of every one, Madison came out in
favor of discrimination; but he admitted
that the certificates must be paid in full;
and proposed a plan for a division between the original holder and the purchaser so hopelessly impracticable, that
he could muster only thirteen votes in
his support. Madison shrank from anything like dishonesty, but he was beginning to break from the friends of the
Constitution and from the party to which
he naturally belonged, because he felt
the drift of Virginian sentiment, and was
not strong enough to withstand the pressure. In this struggle, the supporters of
the secretary, known as the Federalists,
and hitherto acting merely as friends of
the Constitution, first gained real cohe-
sion as a party devoted to a given policy.
Their only opponent of ability was Madison, and his opposition was rendered
abortive and impracticable by his honesty and logic. The debate was long and
heated, but the Federalists, having ability, sound reason, and the advantage of
position on their side, prevailed. They
also carried through the payment of the
arrears of interest. Only one point remained, and that was the crucial test, the
assumption of the state debts. Much had
been done before this point was reached.
Even if Congress went no farther than
they had already gone, the credit of the
country was reasonably safe; but the
policy of the secretary would have been
sadly mutilated. Public credit would not
be rounded and complete; and, above all,
the financial policy would have been deprived of much of its political and constitutional effects upon parties, upon the
strength of the government, and upon

the relations of the States. Sharp as the
battle had been over discrimination in
the payment of the domestic debt, it was
a mere preliminary skirmish compared to
the conflict upon assumption. The lines
were clearly drawn, for Hamilton himself
had marked them out. Parties were marshaled now, not on the acceptance of the
Constitution, but as to the policy of the
government created by the Constitution;
and on the question of assumption they
faced each other for the first vigorous,
well-defined political contest in the history of the United States.

There was no need here to cast about
for popular arguments, as in the case
of the domestic debt, where the real
grounds and objects of opposition were
not clearly conceived, or were better
hidden from view. There was an abund-
ance of subsidiary and obvious arguments brought forward to the effect that
too great a burden would be laid upon
the people; that the state debts could not
with justice be saddled upon the United
States; that assumption was unfair in
benefiting some States largely and not
helping others, and among them some of
the most deserving, at all. All these points
were raised, and local feeling ran very
high, particularly upon the last, leading
to much angry recrimination and comparison of services in the Revolution.
But after all was said, the most vigorous
attack was against the chief purpose of
the secretary, the end which he here had
in view above all others of strengthening
the national government by this large
increase of its creditors, transferring the
interest of a powerful class from the
States to the Union, and in this way
binding the States closer together and
weakening enormously the vigor of the
state-rights sentiments. Politically it was
a bold and masterly stroke, but Hamilton's opponents saw at what it aimed as

plainly as he did himself. A loud cry went up against this centralizing movement. The anti-Federalists, with reviving dislike of the Constitution, felt with sudden keenness the strength and pressure of the bonds which the minister of finance was drawing closer and closer about the people and the States, and they struggled desperately to get free.

Hamilton had foreseen this opposition, but he had reckoned on certain forces to sustain him, and he did not reckon in vain. His first ally was the enthusiasm aroused by his own policy; his second, the confidence and interest of the capitalists and merchants; his third, the direct pecuniary gain to certain States in the success of assumption; and his fourth and most important, the powerful body of able men in and out of Congress who desired a strong central government, whose objects were the same as his own, and who had found in him a leader about whom they could gather in solid phalanx. These forces prevailed. After a long and heated conflict, assumption was carried in committee of the whole, but the majority, although compact and unyielding, was narrow. Delay served the opposition well. When the resolutions got out of committee and came up in the House, the members from North Carolina, at last in the Union, had taken their seats, and they turned the scale against assumption. By their aid the resolution was recommitted, and the Federalists, determined to have all or nothing, sent the rest of the measures back with it. Again the party opposed to assumption prevailed, and the whole policy was at a stand. Feeling ran very high, and ugly murmurs of dissolution began to be heard. It looked as if the measures, destined above all others to consolidate the new Union, would wreck it at the very start. Hamilton had summoned his spirits, and they

had come to him. All the forces he had calculated upon had responded and done their work, but a new factor had been introduced and they could do no more. The dead-lock was as perilous as it was unforseen, but the adverse majority was very small, only two votes, and Hamilton was not only determined but fertile in resources. He would not yield one jot of his financial policy, but he was perfectly ready to give up something else; and in the site of the new capital, the federal city, he found a suitable victim for the sacrifice.

This matter of the seat of government had excited great controversy and feeling between States and sections. Whether the future capital should be in New York or Pennsylvania, in Virginia or Maryland; whether this inestimable boon should fall to the North or to the South, was a burning question second only to assumption. Local prejudice and local pride were raised to white heat on this momentous issue. To Hamilton all this was supremely indifferent. Much of his strength and somewhat of his weakness as a public man came from the fact that, while he was purely and intensely national in opinion, and was devotedly attached to the United States, he was utterly devoid of local feeling and of state pride. There is no evidence that he cared one whit, except as a matter of mere abstract convenience, where Congress fixed the site of the federal city; but he was keenly alive to the fact that everybody about him cared a great deal, and whether reasonably or not was of no consequence. The party which favored assumption were, as a rule, on the side of a northern capital, and had prevailed. The party which resisted assumption favored a southern capital, and had been beaten. To gain the necessary votes for assumption Hamilton determined to sacrifice what he justly thought was a perfectly trivial question, and thus save the financial policy which he rightly considered to be of vital importance, and the very corner-stone of the new government. To carry out this scheme he needed the alliance of a Southern leader, and he pitched upon the man fated to become his great opponent, — the leader and type of one school of thought and politics, as Hamilton was himself the leader and type of the other.

Thomas Jefferson had just returned from France and taken his place at the head of Washington's cabinet. He came back with both body and brain dressed in the French fashion. His subtle, ingenious mind was full of the ideas of the French Revolution, then beginning in Paris. But except for his belief in liberty and humanity, which was born with him and which he did not go to Paris to learn, the wild ravings of the Jacobin clubs and the doctrines of Marat and Robespierre were as little a part of the real man as his French clothes. He would use the ideas of French democracy so long as they were useful and a fit covering for his real purposes, and then he would lay them aside as he did his French coat when it was worn out. With his mind thus occupied, Jefferson had come home to an America very different from the one he had left. A new government, with the inception and plan of which he had had but little sympathy, had been constructed, and the foundations of a strong state were already rising among the ruins of the old confederacy. He found a vigorous party, led for the most part by new men, arrayed in defense of a strong central government, and urging forward all measures calculated to invigorate it. Opposed to them were a body of men, numerous, it is true, but scattered and disorganized, with no possible party

ground except resistance to the Constitution and all its works. Jefferson, with his keen perceptions, saw at a glance the folly of opposition to the Constitution; but as he surveyed the field on which he had just arrived it was by no means easy to determine what position to take. Nevertheless, while he waited and watched for developments, he had to do something, and that something, as was most natural, was to give his support to the administration of which he was a part, and to its measures, which then consisted of Hamilton's financial policy, hanging in the balance on the decision of Congress as to assumption. Jefferson saw as plainly as anybody the scope of the financial policy and the intrinsic merit of assumption. He had, moreover, no prejudices at that time against the author of the policy. With no line marked out for his conduct, and ready, until events decided otherwise, to sustain the administration, he fell in easily enough with the schemes of his colleague. There was a little talk and a little dinner, and Hamilton agreed to secure votes for a southern capital, and Jefferson promised to do the same for assumption. It would be an error to treat this as a bargain or compromise between opposing factions, for it was the work of two cabinet ministers favoring the same policy. Hamilton gained success for his great plans. Jefferson by his personal influence helped to carry through the measures of the administration of which he was a member, and obtained in return the concession of the site of the capital, which was of value to him as a Southern leader. In after times, when Hamilton stood to Jefferson and his party as the representative of all that was bad, the memory of this transaction of 1790, and of a friendly alliance with the great Federalist, became troublesome. Jefferson would fain have erased from history the whole business. He wished the world to believe that the wicked, aristocratic, monarchical Federalists had always been his foes, and had found in him their mightiest opponent. Yet there was the ugly fact that he had himself turned the scale in favor of one of their fundamental measures. His manner of dealing with the problem was characteristic. He did not explain it away in his lifetime, for he might have met with awkward contradiction. But he set it all down for the benefit of posterity, and then excused himself for having supported a measure of the administration of which he was a member, and for having aided the accursed Federalists, by saying that he was "duped by Hamilton."

It is impossible to resist pausing over this statement, for it is one of the most amusing ever made even by Jefferson, and shows a confidence in the credulity of posterity which is not flattering. In justice to Jefferson it must be said that, as long as he had made up his mind to get himself out of what he considered a scrape, this was the only excuse he could make. But it was, unluckily, a most clumsy and transparent deception. Thomas Jefferson had his weaknesses and his failings, but an imperfect knowledge of human nature and human character was not among them. In the difficult art of understanding his fellow men he was unrivaled, and he was never deceived by any man, unless by himself and as to his own motives. On the other hand, Hamilton was the very last man to succeed in duping others, and it would be difficult to find anything more impossible to Hamilton than the feat attributed to him by his rival. He had a directness of thought and action which was always remarkable, and at times overbearing and intolerant. It may well be doubted

whether he could have successfully duped any one, even if he had tried, and he certainly had far too much sense to have attempted such an experiment on so unpromising a subject as Jefferson.

But we are indebted to Jefferson, and to his inability to let well alone, for the details of this whole matter, since the other side held their tongues. The Federalists were not, as a party, given to useless chatter, while Hamilton as usual went straight to his mark, called out unexpected resources, and said nothing about it. Congress took up the funding measures again, and the old angry wrangling went on even after a disagreeable consciousness that they were beaten in some unknown way had crept over the opposition. When the decisive moment came, their fears were fully confirmed. The capital went to the Potomac and assumption was voted. The first great battle had now been fought in all its parts and the secretary had won.

The plans for the revenue, for the excise, for the mint, were adopted in principle, and substantially as Hamilton advised. The secretary's innocent suggestion, that the image and symbols on the coins might be made to have an educational bearing, led to a proposal to stamp on one side of the coins the head of the President for the time being. This harmless proposition produced a debate amusing to us, but very earnest, heated, and real a hundred years ago. The upshot of it all was the adoption of the head of Liberty for the coins, and the discussion has no value except as showing the state of public feeling. From this utterly insignificant controversy we see that when Hamilton sought to advance the cause of strong centralized government and of an aristocratic republic he was not crying in the wilderness. He appealed to clearly marked opinions, entertained by a body of men powerful by their talents if not by their numbers. On the other hand, there appears an immense amount of ill-defined sentiment cherished by a majority of the people, but in a party sense ill-regulated and incoherent, which turned longingly back toward the days of a shattered confederacy and sovereign States, which was thoroughly democratic, and looked with morbid suspicion on everything, no matter what, which tended to lend strength or dignity to the central government. It was this opposition which met Hamilton at every point, and which, as it felt his strong hand drawing the bonds of federal and national government more and more tightly, detected aristocracy in every public office, and scented monarchy in the image and superscription of the coins; while among the party of the secretary were to be found those who, with all their wise policy and high purposes, believed forms and titles essential not merely to dignity but to strength. The truth, as usual, lay somewhere between the extremes illustrated by the trifling symbols on which excessive partisans set a high price.

The next really great measure in the financial policy gave rise to a stubborn contest which was carried through both houses of Congress and into the cabinet, there to receive its final decision at the hands of Washington. The opposition, which had been aroused by the assumption of the state debts, to the strengthening and concentrating effect of the financial policy, cried out loudly against the additional bond of union disclosed in the bank. They railed against the class which was thus being bound to the government, and against the capitalists who were being brought to the side of the administration. They pointed out that the South and agriculture were sacrificed to the North and trade. But all was vain.

Hamilton was now on the flood-tide of success, and the national bank passed by a good majority. The most formidable weapon employed against it was the constitutional argument used by Madison, and, as the President was known to have doubts on this point, the last and strongest stand was made in the cabinet. Jefferson, Randolph, and Madison severally gave Washington written arguments against the bank. In great haste and pressed by business, Hamilton made the famous reply which has already been discussed, and which gained Washington's adherence. In defending the bank, Hamilton established the doctrine of the implied powers, — a matter infinitely more potent and more far-reaching than the establishment of the great financial machine which called it forth.

The last of the reports, that on manufactures, was economically more important than any of its predecessors, but it had no immediate results. Congress had already discussed the question vaguely, and had done something to favor home production and American commerce. The question of protection or free trade was constantly in men's minds, but a system was of slow growth. Hamilton pointed to the road to be followed, and other men traveled in it, among the first Jefferson and Madison with their plan of "allowances" for the fisheries, while at the same time they denounced the theory, its author, and all his works, including "protection and bounties." Hamilton marked out clearly and fully a plan for the development of industry, trade, and commerce. He turned the current of thought, he influenced the future, but the task was too mighty, the scheme was too vast to be carried out at once, or in fact otherwise than piecemeal, although its suggestion was a fit termination to the great work which he had accomplished.

Thus was the financial policy completed, adopted, and put in operation as Hamilton designed it. The only mischance was the speculation which began with the debt certificates, was fostered by the success of the bank, and expanded into a wild mania, and consequent panic and disaster. From the outset the secretary had striven to check this spirit, of which he saw the evil and danger. He repelled his friends who sought information, and did all that was possible to cool the excitement. He strove in vain, and then was blamed for the speculation, the rapid fortunes, and the swift disaster alike.

The only miscalculation made by Hamilton was in regard to the rate of interest, which he supposed would fall, but which, owing to the marvelous rapidity of material development and the consequent employment of capital, really rose. The error was almost unavoidable, and it was quite harmless. The criticisms which have been made on this famous series of measures have been various and contradictory. It was said at the time that Hamilton made the debt too permanent, but on the other hand it was also urged that he was putting too great a burden on the people, and the shorter the loan the greater the immediate burden. In this he observed a just mean and a wise moderation. The unexpected rate of growth in the country showed afterwards that the debt might have been paid more rapidly, but at the moment Hamilton's anticipations of revenue were generally regarded as absurdly sanguine. The most forcible criticism, which was made either then or since, was that the financial policy was too strong, that it put too great a strain upon the infant experiment, ventured too much, ran too great a risk, and came near causing shipwreck. Hamilton reasoned that, if his financial policy could be made successful, a good national government might be built up, and that if it proved too strong and the new system gave way, then the Constitution was not worth preserving. Of the soundness of this argument, as it seems to me, there can be no doubt. But after all, the best evidence is in results. There was no public credit. Hamilton created it. There was no circulating medium, no financial machinery; he supplied them. Business was languishing, and business revived under the treasury measures. There was no government, no system with life in it, only a paper constitution. Hamilton exercised the powers granted by the Constitution, pointed out those which lay hidden in its dry clauses, and gave vitality to the lifeless instrument. He drew out the resources of the country, he exercised the powers of the Constitution, he gave courage to the people, he laid the foundations of national government — and this was the meaning and result of the financial policy.

Irving Brant: SPECULATORS vs. VETERANS

"MAY I ask of your friendship," wrote Alexander Hamilton to Madison on October 12, 1789, "to put to paper and send me your thoughts on such objects as may have occurred to you for an addition to our revenue, and also as to any modifications of the public debt, which could be made consistent with good faith — the interest of the public and of its creditors?"

Hamilton made this request in response to a parting note and the loan of a book when Madison left for Virginia. In reply came these suggestions: An excise on home distilleries, with the tax regulated by the size of the still to avoid vexatious searches; higher duties on imported liquor; a land tax, getting ahead of the states in this field; a stamp tax on federal court proceedings large enough to make the judiciary support itself.

Madison had formed no precise ideas on the public debt. Everybody expected the foreign part to be put on a sound footing. Would it not be soothing to those unfavorably disposed if the domestic debt could be lessened by purchases on public account, particularly by means of western land sales? The debt ought to be extinguished. Many, he knew, were in favor of prolonging or even perpetuating it. He was opposed to this because the people disrelished the idea, also a long-term debt would slide into the hands of foreigners. He closed with affectionate regards, the last that ever passed in either direction between them.[1]

Hamilton's Report on Public Credit[2] carried revenue provisions similar to those Madison suggested, but that was incidental. It revealed a national debt of $54,124,464.56, nearly all growing out of the Revolutionary War. The foreign debt (including $1,600,000 of defaulted interest) amounted to $11,700,000. The $42,000,000 domestic debt included overdue interest of $13,000,000. The great bulk of it consisted of six-per-cent certificates issued to settle army pay and farmers' and contractors' claims for war supplies and services. Other certificates covered wartime loans by citizens and continental currency redeemed after its forty-for-one devaluation in 1780. An unliquidated debt of $2,000,000 was the value Hamilton placed on about $80,000,000 of old currency still outstanding. (Redeemed later at 100 for one.)

Knowing the American dislike of taxes, the Treasury chief delivered a basic lecture on the need to lift national credit by punctual performance of contracts. The soaring prices of public securities testified to a belief that this would be done, and "the most enlightened friends of good government are those whose expectations are the highest." A proper provision for public credit would win their confidence and cement more closely the union of the states. Public securities

[1] Hamilton to Madison, October 12, 1789. Madison to Hamilton, November 19, 1789. Hamilton, *History of the Republic*, IV, 60–64. (Published there with added italics.) Hamilton Papers, VIII, 999 (LC).

[2] *Annals of the Congress of the United States*, II, 1991–2021. Hamilton, *Works* (Lodge), II, 227–289.

From *James Madison: Father of the Constitution, 1787–1800* by Irving Brant, copyright 1950, pp. 290–305, used by special permission of the publishers, The Bobbs-Merrill Company.

would then become a virtual part of the money system, promoting national prosperity.

There were other ways of stating these things. Previous to the making of the report, Madison wrote, the avidity of speculators sent prices up from a few shillings to eight or ten in the pound, "and emissaries are still exploring the interior and distant parts of the Union in order to take advantage of the ignorance of holders."[3] Bluntly stated, Hamilton's precept was: Bind the rich to the government by self-interest.

This brought the Secretary to the storm center of his report. More than once he had read that a discrimination ought to be made between original holders of public securities and those who had bought them at a depreciated price. That would be a breach of contract and would ruin public credit. If the losses of the original holders were to be made up, their claim was against the government.

There is nothing to indicate whether Madison ever discussed this subject with Hamilton in their occasional talks and rambles in New York. No hint of it, certainly, is to be found in the recorded recollections of an old dame who, as a girl, saw them "talk together in the summer, and then turn, and laugh, and play with a monkey that was climbing in a neighbor's yard."[4] Nevertheless, the Secretary thought it wise to buttress his case with the address to the states which Madison wrote for the old Congress in 1783. It would be unnecessary and invidious, said that paper, to discriminate between those who originally made loans to the government and those who showed confidence by receiving transfers.

For the refunding of the domestic debt,

creditors were to be given their choice of long-term or lifetime annuities, provided they would agree to a reduction of interest from six to four per cent. In theory the exchange was voluntary, but those who clung to their six-per-cent bonds were to receive no more interest than the others. Hamilton expected by this means to reduce the annual cost of the debt from $4,600,000 to $2,240,000. The "cement to the Union" would stick for at least forty years.

Finally, the Secretary asked that the federal government take over the debts, estimated at $25,000,000, incurred by the states during the Revolution. He said it was wrong to distinguish between local and general defense, but his main object, stated privately, was to tie state creditors to the national government.[5]

Assumption of state debts originated with Madison in 1783, but Congress struck it out of his revenue plan. This background made Hamilton confident of Madison's support, without full reason. The latter wanted assumption in order to win ratification of the federal impost. That issue was dead, and the state securities, like the federal, were passing into the hands of big speculators.

From every quarter came reports about the buying up of federal certificates. Senator Maclay heard that Robert Morris' New York partner, William Constable, had one contract for forty thousand dollars' worth. Boston people were involved. "Indeed, there is no room to doubt but a connection is spread over the whole continent on this villainous business."

Newly arrived Senator Hawkins of North Carolina reported that he passed two expresses with great sums of money on their way south. Wadsworth (Con-

[3] Madison to Jefferson, January 24, 1790.

[4] Hamilton, *History of the Republic*, IV, 29n.

[5] Hamilton to Carrington, May 26, 1792.

necticut congressman) had sent off two money-laden vessels. Other members of Congress were reported deep in the business. Nobody doubted that the speculative commotion originated from the Treasury. Most people blamed Assistant Secretary Duer, but Maclay believed it stemmed from Hamilton.[6]

Madison took no part in the early debate on Hamilton's report. Jackson wanted action postponed so that the speculators would burn their fingers. Gerry, Sedgwick and others called for quick action. Speculation was inevitable, even useful, they argued, and the only way to end it was to bring securities up to their face value. Smith, reported to have sent a money ship south, moved that no discrimination be made between original holders and assignees. Scott and Livermore called for devaluation of the debt. It was inflated paper issued to pay for goods and services at extravagant prices — not even an obligation of the government, but an old claim of one part of the people against the whole of them. Scott's motion was beaten, whereupon Burke moved a discrimination but withdrew his motion before debate, saying he did not favor it. That brought Madison to the floor.

Anxious to profit from the thoughts of others, he had chosen to be a listener, but the turn affairs had taken required him to speak now if at all. The debt, he affirmed, was fully valid. By whom was it contracted? By the United States in a national capacity, by the government as agent of the whole people.

The change in the government which has taken place has enlarged its national capacity, but it has not varied the national obligation, with respect to the engagements entered into by that transaction. . . . Although the

[6] Maclay, January 15, 18, 1790.

government has been changed the nation remains the same . . . the obligation remains the same.

What then was the amount of the debt? It was the amount the United States received and had promised to pay. No logic, no magic, could diminish it. "The only point on which we can deliberate is, to whom the payment is really due." There were, said Madison, four classes proper to notice:

Original creditors who still held their securities.

Original creditors who had alienated them.

Present holders of alienated securities.

Intermediate holders, who had acquired securities but no longer held them.

The first group was entitled to full payment. The fourth should be dismissed offhand. The second and third groups — the original and present holders of alienated securities — had rival pretensions.

The second group, Madison believed, had a claim in which humanity reinforced justice. The value they delivered to the government had never been repaid to them. The securities they were forced to receive had less real value, even at the time of issuance, than the sums due. The debt was not extinguished. The sufferings of the soldiers could never be forgotten while sympathy was an American virtue — to say nothing of the injustice of requiring those who lost seven eights of their due to contribute to those who made a sevenfold gain.

Holders by assignment, he continued, had a valid claim upon the public faith. The two sets of claims interfered. That being the case, they must either pay both, reject one, or make a composition between them. To pay both would far exceed the value received by the public. To reject wholly the claims of the assignees would be fatal to public credit. To load the entire loss on the other group was an idea at which human nature recoiled.

A composition then is the only expedient that remains; let it be a liberal one in favor of the present holders, let them have the highest price which has prevailed in the market; and let the residue belong to the original sufferers.

By this plan, all but a few of the present holders would make a profit. The others would lose nothing and would get a sound six-per-cent investment. It would be said the plan was impracticable. But all it required was a knowledge of the present holders, which was shown by the certificates, and of the original holders, whose names were in office documents. Some might say it would injure public credit. That would be prevented by the honesty and disinterestedness of the policy, which would not save the government a farthing — also by full provision for the foreign debt and punctuality in future domestic payments.

The present case was so extraordinary, it seemed to Madison, that ordinary maxims could not be applied to it. The American situation was like that of England in the South Sea scheme, where a thousand-per-cent change in the value of stock produced government interference. If the condition existing in American national securities were to happen among individuals a court of equity would interpose to give redress.

If a tribunal existed on earth, by which nations could be compelled to do right, the United States would be compelled to do something not dissimilar in its principles to what I have contended for.[7]

[7] *Annals*, January 28, February 8, 9, 10, 11, 1790.

Madison then offered a motion for discrimination and the 1790 fight was on. Nobody denied the injustice suffered by the original holders. With Boudinot leading off and Sedgwick, Ames, Smith and Laurance adding their weight, the opponents argued that nothing could be done about these losses. The instant a claimant assigned his claim, he was through. It was not even possible to discover who were the real first holders, since innumerable certificates were issued in the names of government clerks. To attempt a refund would lay a foundation for frauds and perjuries. "Do not rob on the highway to exercise charity," cried Ames. Madison's measure would destroy the property and faith of foreign investors, violate the sacred rights of property, duplicate the evils of state tender laws, produce confusion, corruption and expense. Ames would not charge Madison with a deliberate intent to produce these mischiefs:

I think so highly of his probity and patriotism that if he can be made to see that these consequences will follow, or only be apprehended, he will give up his scheme. But if government has this right, what right of private property is safe?

Arguments based on sympathy for veterans and dislike of speculators did not seem so bad to Jackson of Georgia, Seney of Maryland, White, Page and Lee of Virginia. Soldiers had been forced to receive certificates with a current value, when received, of two shillings sixpence for a twenty-shilling note. It was said now that they should have held onto them. And leave their children to starve on a dunghill?

This drew no tears from Livermore. "Esau had sold his birthright for a mess of pottage, and heaven and earth had confirmed the sale." That remark boded ill for Madison's motion. The New Hampshire man and several others were eager to scale down the domestic debt in order to cut taxes. If it must be paid in full, why worry over who was to get the money?[8]

Taking the floor again on February 18, Madison refused to admit "that America ought to erect the monuments of her gratitude, not to those who saved her liberties, but to those who had enriched themselves in her funds." Claimants entitled to receive gold or silver had been given a piece of paper worth at the moment of delivery one eighth of its face value.

Was this depreciated paper freely accepted? No. The government offered that or nothing. . . . The same degree of constraint would vitiate a transaction between man and man before any court of equity on the face of the earth.

The speaker said he had been criticized for appealing to the heart as well as the head. He would be bold to repeat that in great and unusual questions of morality the heart was the better judge. Gentlemen should consider "not the form, but the substance — not the letter, but the equity — not the bark, but the pith of the business."

Opposition speakers had reminded Madison repeatedly of his authorship of the address of Congress which rejected a discrimination. At that period, he replied, the certificates to the army and citizens at large had not been issued. Transfers, few in number and entailing little loss, were confined to loan-office certificates.

At present, the transfers extend to a vast proportion of the whole debt, and the loss to

[8] *Annals,* February 11, 15, 16, 17, 18, 19, 1790.

the original holders has been immense. The injustice which has taken place has been enormous and flagrant, and makes redress a great national object.

This change of circumstances, Madison insisted, destroyed the argument from the act of 1783. But if it were to be adhered to implicitly, how could anybody justify the compulsory reduction of interest called for in the Treasury plan? He denied that one set of men was to be robbed to pay another. If there had been robbery, it was committed on the original holders. He wished a part to be withheld from each of two creditors, both of whom could not be paid the whole. The audience was enlarged at this point by an influx on the floor which Maclay tells about:

The Senate now adjourned and we went into the lower House to hear the debates on Mr. Madison's motion. Madison had been up most of the morning and was said to have spoken most ably indeed. He seemed rather jaded when I came in. He had, early in the business, been called on to show a single instance where anything like the present had been done. He produced an act of Parliament in point in the reign of Queen Anne. But now the gentlemen [Laurance and Ames] quitted this ground and cried out for rigid right on law principles. Madison modestly put them in mind that they had challenged him on this ground and he had met them agreeably to their wishes.

Benson wanted to know whether an original creditor who had assigned his certificate could, in conscience, accept a reimbursement in the manner proposed. In general, Madison answered, assignments were made with reference to market value and the uncertainty of government policies. No scruples could arise out of that. In turn he would ask whether a present holder who got his certificate from a distressed fellow citizen for one tenth of its ultimate value might not feel some remorse in retaining so unconscionable an advantage. The embarrassed Benson could reply only that if a soldier made such an application to him as a matter of right, he would reject it, but if his benevolence were appealed to — what he would do would depend on other principles.

Madison showed that the Treasury plan cut the interest on the liquidated debt and violated the pledge of redemption written on the face of the old currency. If contracts were immutable, all should be enforced. If not, Congress should attend to the correction of injustice. There were difficulties, but the true ownership of securities could be traced. There would be more frauds and perjuries in the collection of duties than were likely in this case. Devote the same ingenuity to removing difficulties that was employed in raising them and they would vanish.

Expecting Madison's motion to be defeated, Senator Maclay sought him out at his lodgings on the day the vote was to be taken. It had occurred to the Pennsylvanian that he could offer a good deal of useful guidance. House Clerk Beckley, he noted in his journal, was very intimate both with Speaker Muhlenberg and with Madison.

I can, through this channel, communicate what I please to Madison; and I think I know him. But if he is led, it must be without letting him know that he is so; in other words, he must not see the string.

Maclay's suggestion was simple — slash interest to three per cent and pay everything by making debt certificates and nothing else receivable in sales of public lands. The senator had taken his plan to Congressman Scott, who declared that if Madison would join it could be carried. "I wished him to communicate with Madison. He was afraid of Madison's pride." It was at Scott's suggestion that Maclay called on Madison and read the resolutions to him, first telling him with typical delicacy that his own proposition hadn't a chance to succeed.

It hurt his *Littleness*. I do not think he believed me. I read the resolutions. I do not think he attended to one word of them, so much did he seem absorbed in his own ideas. I put them into his hand. He offered them back without reading them. . . . His pride seems of that kind which repels all communication. . . . The obstinacy of this man has ruined the opposition.

To those who wanted to scale the debt or defeat the funding of it, Madison's attitude might indeed seem obstinate and full of pride. What he desired was a fair distribution of what the government was to pay, not an escape from paying it. The pious land speculator, Manasseh Cutler, was in the gallery when the vote was taken on February 22. For a week, he wrote, the House had been debating a very unexpected motion by Mr. Madison — a motion which would have been smiled at had it come from a member of less consequence, "but his character gave it importance. . . . On taking the question, Mr. M. had the mortification, which he appeared sensibly to feel, to be in a minority — only thirteen for the motion."[9]

The thirteen-to-thirty-six vote was far more one-sided than Madison's advance estimate. Nine Virginians and four other

[9] *Annals*, February 18, 19, 22, 1790. Maclay, January 17, February 18, 21, 22, 1790. M. Cutler to Oliver Everett, February 24, 1790, Cutler, I, 458.

Southerners supported his motion. The causes of this, he wrote to Randolph, could not altogether be explained, and some of them he preferred to discuss orally. Actually he faced a five-way combination: congressional speculators, cementers of the rich, those who feared injury to public credit, those who thought a revision desirable but impracticable, those who preferred Hamilton's plan because it scaled the debt by reducing interest. The political weakness of Madison's position lay in the fact that the justice he called for would hurt the rich, help the poor and save nothing to the taxpayer.[10]

Unshaken, he wrote to his father that his proposition was much better relished in the country at large than in New York. Abigail Adams thought he was "acting a covered and artful part." Youthful John Quincy Adams reported that Madison's reputation had suffered from his conduct, Judge Dana being his only respectable Boston supporter. It was a nonrespectable one who wrote in the *Columbian Centinel*: "Happy there is a Madison who fearless of the blood suckers will step forward and boldly vindicate the rights of the widows and orphans, the original creditors and the war worn soldier." Anger and cynicism stirred other good men to bad poetry, such as these newspaper lines "On the rejection of Mr. Madison's motion":

"Pay the poor soldier! — He's a sot,"
Cries our grave ruler B-ud-not.
"No pity, *now*, from us he claims,"
In artful accents, echoes Am-s:
"In *war*, to heroes let's be just,
In *peace*, we'll write their toils in dust;
A soldier's pay are rags and fame,
A wooden leg — a deathless name.
To Specs, both *in* and *out* of Cong,
The four and six per cents belong."[11]

Throughout this business, Madison informed a critic, he had carefully refrained from attacking the title of the actual holders of securities because he did not wish to influence popular prejudices. He nevertheless believed that in many instances the purchases had been vitiated by fraud or impaired by lack of a valuable consideration. Finally, he doubted whether the buyer was more entitled than the seller to the benefits resulting from establishment of the new government — an event "as much out of the contemplation of both parties as a miraculous shower of gold from heaven."[12] His own and later generations have agreed on the sincerity of Madison's motives in proposing a discrimination among security holders. Three factors, however, have interfered with recognition of the rightness and wisdom of his proposal:

1. His deliberate understatement of his own case to avoid stirring up an already excited public.

2. Failure to realize that public credit was restored by the setting up of a strong government with taxing power, rather than by the specific nature of the plan adopted, which violently impaired contracts by cutting part of the interest to three per cent and deferring another part until 1800.

3. The vagueness of the charges about wholesale speculation by government officials and other insiders.

The influence of the first factor is self-evident. A hint of the second came from

son to Randolph, March 14, 1790. Madison to James Madison, Sr., February 27, 1790. Abigail Adams to Cotton Tufts, March 7, 1790 (Henkels Catalog, May 13, 1937). J. Q. Adams to J. Adams, April 5, 1790. *Columbian Centinel*, February 24, 1790. *Pennsylvania Gazette*, March 24, 1790.

10 Madison to Randolph, March 14, 1790.
11 Madison to Pendleton, March 4, 1790. Madi-

12 Madison to unknown, March 14, 1790, Emmet Papers (NYPL).

Maclay, who complained that Madison's system did not reduce the burden, but distributed the benefits more fairly, and was, perhaps, "on that account more dangerous, as it will be readier submitted to." The third handicap — vagueness of the speculation charges — can be removed.

The day before Madison delivered his principal speech on discrimination he received an anonymous letter signed "Foreigner." After giving an account of European purchases the writer forgot his origin and drew on personal knowledge of Revolutionary finance to combat Madison's charge of injustice to veterans. The only person who could have marshaled that particular combination of facts and perversions was William Duer, Hamilton's assistant, who had been secretary of the old Board of Treasury.

Certain agents, his story ran, offered to contract with Hollanders to furnish a large amount of the domestic debt of the United States. The careful Dutch wanted assurance against discrimination, so "the secretary of the Board of Treasury under the seal of his office gave attestation to confirm the facts." Great amounts were purchased by Dutch bankers at fifteen shillings in the pound. The bankers then issued "actions"— little notes backed by the American securities — and sold these at higher prices (at or near par) to thousands of Dutch investors. If Madison's amendment should prevail European faith in America would be shattered.[13]

Who were the "certain agents" who contracted to deliver these securities? For that, read a memorandum dated December 21, 1788, in the papers of Rufus King. "Some days since," King recorded, "Colonel Duer mentioned to me that his situation required that he should

pay some attention to his pecuniary concerns." A Geneva banker, M. de Claviere, approaching through Brissot de Warville, wanted him and other Americans to join in buying up the American debt to France. Duer "told me that he had conferred with Wadsworth, General Knox and Mr. Osgood [member of the Treasury Board] on the subject — that he had informed them that Robert and Gouverneur Morris . . . proposed to unite with him (Duer) and that Gouverneur Morris was going to Europe with this among other views."

The design was "that Duer, Robert Morris and Gouverneur Morris should be the principal Americans, that Constable and Duer's friend (Osgood) should be admitted," along with some others who could not be left out, and the three principals should split all profits above those of the limited shareholders. Should this fail, the idea was to accomplish the measure through an American minister in Holland. Duer invited King to enter the speculation and said that Knox and Wadsworth wished to know whether he would accept an appointment to Holland. King gave an ambiguous answer on the first point, but told Duer that he was not indisposed to a foreign appointment. It would be a great satisfaction to promote the interest of his friends if he could do so with propriety, but the opinions of Jay and Hamilton were of consequence. "Previous to any decision on my part I must be ascertained of their opinions."[14]

Gouverneur Morris went to Europe bearing letters from Duer (so said King) to promote the speculation. Madison gave him a letter of introduction to Jefferson with this note added in cipher: "I am a stranger to the errand on which G. Morris goes to Europe. It relates, I presume, to the affairs of R. Morris, which

---

[13] Maclay, February 19, 1790. "Foreigner" to Madison, February 17, 1790 (NYPL).

[14] R. King, Memorandum, December 21, 1788, King Papers.

are still much deranged." Nothing came
of the French scheme, but Holland produced a flourishing alternative in speculative purchases of American securities.
Jefferson, going to Amsterdam to borrow
money with which to meet interest on
the *foreign* debt, protested to the Board
of Treasury that Dutch purchasers of the
domestic debt made this impossible.
What banker would pay ninety-six per
cent for one public security when he
could buy another of the same nation for
fifty-five per cent? The Stanitzky house,
he reported, held $1,340,000 of the
American domestic debt and was trying
to blackmail the United States by refusing to service the foreign debt unless
paid a year's interest on its domestic
securities. Little did Jefferson suspect
that his bitter complaints went straight
to the chief American organizer of the
European speculations, soon to become
Hamilton's principal assistant.[15]

In all that followed there is no hint
that Hamilton stood to make a dollar,
but King's memorandum leaves no doubt
that he knew exactly what Duer was,
and what he was doing and likely to do,
when he chose him in September 1789
to be assistant secretary of the Treasury.
What Duer proceeded to do is recorded
over his own signature in a "Memorandum of agreement made and entered into
the 23 of December 1789 between William Duer and William Constable both
of New York." Signed by both parties
before a witness, and preserved in Constable's papers, this contract between
Hamilton's chief assistant and New
York's leading financier begins as follows:

The parties having full confidence in each
other agree to enter into a speculation in the
funds generally to create a capital for which
object it is proposed to purchase on time as
many continental securities as can be obtained, the money arising therefrom to be
immediately invested in the debts of North
and South Carolina to the extent of sixteen
thousand specie dollars, the residue in indents of interest or such other paper as may
be determined on.

This speculation was far more ambitious than the reference to $16,000 indi-
cates. Borrowing on what they bought
and pyramiding their loans, they could
hope for a tremendous profit through
the rise of security prices when the
funding plan came into effect. Success
depended on two things — advance
knowledge, which Duer possessed, that
assumption of state funds was to be part
of the Hamilton program; and ignorance
of that fact by the Carolina security holders. December 1789 was late, but Duer's
agents had been in the field since July,
inquiring after securities and concealing
their real object by holding up "the idea
of purchasing rights to lands." There is
nothing to show the total operations of
Duer and Constable, but their certificate
account with Richard Platt has a maxi-
mum figure of $170,114.65 for activities
in which he shared.[16]

Really big speculations could be
financed only in Europe. To bring in
Amsterdam bankers risks must be passed
along to Dutch farmers, mechanics and
widows. That called for long-term paper
in small denominations, with interest
sustained over the whole term of the
speculation. Constable worked that out

15 Madison to Jefferson, December 8, 1788. Jefferson to Board of Treasury, February 7, March
29, 1788 (MS of March 29 letter in Duer Papers,
NYHS). Jefferson to J. Adams, February 6,
1788.

16 Duer-Constable contract, December 23, 1789,
Constable-Pierrepont Papers, Misc. (NYPL).
Duer-Constable-Platt certificate account, *ibid.*
William Steele to W. Duer, July 27, 1789, Duer
Papers (NYHS).

and put his scheme on paper in these words:

Suppose one million of dollars in the debt of South Carolina to be purchased at two shillings in the pound. Suppose the "actions" to be disposed of at 80 per cent, security to be given for the punctual payment of interest at 5 per cent on these "actions."

After deducting the original cost of the purchase, the balance remaining to be placed in the British or other equally solid fund, bearing interest at 4 per cent.

The deficiency of the interest payable annually on the "actions" to be taken from this capital — what would be the result?

The answer was satisfactory. The million-dollar state debt would cost $100,000, but could be handled with $20,000 "as certificates would be transmitted and disposed of to raise funds for discharge of our drafts." The "actions," payable at the Peter Stanitzky banking house in Amsterdam, would bring in $800,000. Deduct the full cost of the collateral, $100,000, and it would leave $700,000 to be invested in British bonds. For the first year, Constable's group would owe $50,000 interest in Holland and receive $28,000 interest in England. They would have to sell $22,000 of the British bonds to make up the deficit. In the fourteenth year the interest payable in Holland would still be $50,000, the interest received in England would be only $13,367, and it would be necessary to sell $36,633 of the shrinking British capital. By that time the state securities were sure to reach par, sale of them would pay off the Amsterdam "actions" and the speculators would still have $297,558 in British bonds — their profit on an original capital of $20,000. The speculators risked little, the bankers nothing. The risk was to be borne by

hundreds of Dutch burghers who were to put up $800,000 for state bonds with a market value of $100,000.

Constable's papers do not show whether this precise plan was put into effect. But when he made a list of his foreign obligations on August 16, 1790, at the height of his speculative activities, the Stanitzky house was in for $840,000, Gerrit Nutches and others for $2,156,479.32, Etienne Lespinasse and others $700,000. The grand total was $5,447,042.27.[17]

This was the cold reality behind Hamilton's plea that good faith, honor and public credit forbade a partial restitution of losses to soldiers of the Revolution out of the profits of assignees — or, to state it another way, behind his plan to make the self-interest of the rich a cement to the Union. Speculation in public funds was not merely the automatic pay-off of past transfers, or the result of a spontaneous rush of gamblers. It was the planned work of international syndicates of European bankers and American politicians and financiers, operating in millions of dollars, with the second highest officer of the United States Treasury as organizer and manager of the most brazen part of the speculation.

Rumor, planting itself in Maclay's journal, could put down a comment on "Wadsworth with his boatload of money," or assert that Constable early in 1790 cleared $35,000 on a contract for $70,000.[18] The closed pages of account and memorandum books concealed the record of a multi-million-dollar conspiracy of bankers and politicians to draw huge unearned profits out of the trust-

[17] William Constable, Memorandum, Constable-Pierrepont Papers, misc. Constable, list of foreign holders, *ibid.*

[18] Maclay, January 18, July 17, 1790.

fulness of Dutchmen and the ignorance of American soldiers and farmers — with the speculators headed by Hamilton's chief assistant and basing their actions on advance knowledge of the plans to be laid before Congress.

James Madison had no knowledge of the Duer-Constable contract, or of the conspiratorial terms under which American speculators fed securities into the financial houses of Commeline, Lespinasse, Nutches, Stanitzky, Willink and other Dutch and Flemish participants in the exploitation of the public debt. He *did* know that clever men were using the Hamilton funding plan to rob their fellow citizens, and the knowledge drove him into political revolt against the financial machine that was taking over the government.

Madison sacrificed his congressional leadership when he undertook the fight for Revolutionary War veterans and other small creditors against speculators in and out of Congress. By the same course he split the original Federalists asunder, fused one part of them with the radical wing of the vanishing Antifederalists and gave direction to the political cleavage which swiftly divided the American public into Federalists and Republicans. Had he possessed personal glamour the next political phenomenon in America would have become known as Madisonian democracy. As it was, he planted the seed and started the growth of the party which received the Jeffersonian label. He did this before Jefferson reentered the national scene from his diplomatic exile.

Vernon Louis Parrington:

ALEXANDER HAMILTON AND THE LEVIATHAN STATE

OF the disciplined forces that put to rout the disorganized party of agrarianism, the intellectual leader was Alexander Hamilton, the brilliant Anglo-French West Indian, then just entered upon his thirties. A man of quite remarkable ability, a lucid thinker, a great lawyer, a skillful executive, a masterly organizer, a statesman of broad comprehension and inflexible purpose, he originated and directed the main policies of the Federalist group, and brought them to successful issue. For this work he was singularly well equipped, for in addition to great qualities of mind and persuasive ways he was free to work unhampered by the narrow localisms and sectional prejudices that hampered native Americans. He was rather English than American, with a certain detachment that refused to permit his large plans to be thwarted by minor, vexatious details, or the perversity of stupid men. He was like the elder Pitt in the magnificence of his imperial outlook.

Such a man would think in terms of the nation rather than of the state. He would agree with Paine that the continental belt must be more securely buckled. The jealousies and rivalries that obstructed the creation of a centralized Federal government found no sympathy with him. He was annoyed beyond all patience with the dissensions of local home rule. In his political philosophy there was no place for "the political monster of an *imperium in imperio*"; he would destroy all lesser sovereignties and reduce the several commonwealths to a parish status. For town-meeting democracies and agrarian legislatures he had frank contempt. The American villager and farmer he never knew and never understood; his America was the America of landed gentlemen and wealthy merchants and prosperous professional men, the classes that were most bitterly anti-agrarian. And it was in association with this group of conservative representatives of business and society that he took his place as directing head in the work of reorganizing the loose confederation into a strong and cohesive union. When that work was accomplished his influence was commanding, and for a dozen years he directed the major policies of the Federalist party. His strategic position as Secretary of the Treasury enabled him to stamp his principles so deeply upon the national economy that in all the intervening years since he quitted his post they have not been permanently altered. That we still follow the broad principles of Hamilton in our financial policy is a remarkable testimony to the perspicacity of his mind and his understanding of the economic forces that control modern society. And hence,

because the Hamiltonian principles lie at the core of the problem which has proved so difficult of solution by modern liberalism, the life and work of Hamilton are of particular significance in our democratic development.

Hamilton was our first great master of modern finance, of that finespun web of credit which holds together our industrial life; and because his policies opened opportunities of profit to some and entailed loss upon others, they have been debated with an acrimony such as few programs have endured. About the figure of the brilliant Federalist the mythmakers have industriously woven their tales, distorting the man into either a demigod or a monster. The individual has been merged in the system which he created, and later interpretation has been shot through with partisan feeling; political and economic prejudice has proved too strong for disinterested estimate. Any rational judgment of Hamilton is dependent upon an interpretation of the historical background that determined his career, and in particular of the state of post-Revolutionary economics; and over such vexing questions partisans have wrangled interminably. Thus Sumner, in his life of Hamilton, asserts dogmatically that Federalism was no other than the forces of law and order at war with the turbulent, anarchistic forces unloosed by the Revolution, and that the putting down of the scheme of repudiation was the necessary preliminary to the establishment of a great nation. In the light of such an interpretation, Hamilton the far-seeing, courageous and honest master of finance, was the savior of nationality, the one supreme figure rising above an envious group of lesser men. But, as has been sufficiently pointed out in preceding chapters, the historical facts are susceptible of quite other interpretation;

and as our knowledge of the economic struggle then going on becomes more adequate, the falsity of such an explanation becomes patent. If, on the other hand, we concede that the crux of the political problem in 1787 was economic — the struggle waging between farmer and business groups for control of government — then the position of Hamilton becomes clear; he was the spokesman of the business economy. He thought in terms of nationality and espoused the economics of capitalism, because he discovered in them potentialities congenial to his imperialistic mind.

The career of Hamilton followed logically from the determining facts of temperament and experience. He came to New York an alien, without position or influence, ambitious to make a name and stir in the world; and in the America of his day there could be little doubt what doors opened widest to preferment. He made friends easily, and with his aristocratic tastes he preferred the rich and distinguished to plebeians. Endowed with charming manners and brilliant parts, he fascinated all whom he met; before he was of age he was intimate with all the Whig leaders, civil and military, on Washington's staff and elsewhere, lending his brains to the solution of knotty problems, prodding stupider minds with illuminating suggestions, proving himself the clearest thinker in whatever group he found himself. It was by sheer force of intellect that he gained distinction. Singularly precocious, he matured early; before his twenty-fifth year he seems to have developed every main principle of his political and economic philosophy, and thereafter he never hesitated or swerved from his path. He was tireless in propaganda, urging on the proposed Constitutional convention, discussing with Robert Morris his favorite project of a national bank, outlining vari-

ous systems of funding, advocating tariffs as an aid to domestic manufacture, and sketching the plan of a political and economic system under which native commercialism could go forward. His reputation as an acute and trustworthy financial adviser was well established with influential men north and south, when the new government was set up, and Washington turned to him naturally for the Treasury post, to guide financial policies during the difficult days immediately ahead. But so able a man could not be restricted within a single portfolio, and during the larger part of Washington's two administrations Hamilton's was the directing mind and chief influence. He regarded himself as Prime Minister and rode roughshod over his colleagues. Major policies such as that of no entangling alliances must receive his careful scrutiny and approval before they were announced; and in consequence more credit belongs to Hamilton for the success of those first administrations than is commonly recognized.

But when we turn from the administrator and statesman to the creative thinker, there is another story to tell. The quickness of his perceptions, the largeness of his plans and efficacy of his methods — his clear brilliancy of understanding and execution — are enormously impressive; but they cannot conceal certain intellectual shortcomings. There was a lack of subtlety in the swift working of his mind, of shades and *nuances* in the background of his thought, that implied a lack of depth and richness in his intellectual accumulation. Something hard, almost brutal lurks in his thought — a note of intellectual arrogance, of cynical contempt. He was utterly devoid of sentiment, and without a shred of idealism, unless a certain grandiose quality in his conceptions be accounted idealism. His absorbing interest in the rising system of credit and finance, his cool unconcern for the social consequences of his policies, reveal his weakness. In spite of his brilliancy Hamilton was circumscribed by the limitations of the practical man.

In consequence of such limitations Hamilton was not a political philosopher in the large meaning of the term. In knowledge of history he does not compare with John Adams; and as an open-minded student of politics he is immensely inferior to Jefferson. Outside the domain of the law, his knowledge does not always keep pace with his argument. He reasons adroitly from given premises, but he rarely pauses to examine the validity of those premises. The fundamentals of political theory he seems never to have questioned, and he lays down a major principle with the easy finality of a dogmatist. Compare his views on any important political principle with those of the greater thinkers of his time, and they are likely to prove factional if not reactionary. The two tests of eighteenth-century liberalism were the doctrine of individualism, and the doctrine of the minimized state; and Hamilton rejected both: the former in its larger social bearing, and the latter wholly. He was not even abreast of seventeenth-century liberalism, for that was strongly republican, and Hamilton detested republicanism only a little less than democracy. Harrington and Locke were no masters of his; much less were Bentham or Priestley or Godwin. He called the French revolutionary writers "fanatics in political science"; to what extent he read them does not appear. The thinkers to whom he owed most seem to have been Hume, from whom he may have derived his cynical psychology, and Hobbes whose absolute state was so congenial to his temperament. But political theory he subordinated to economic theory. He was much interested in economics. With the Physiocratic school and its agrarian and sociological bias he could have no sympathy, but with the rising English school that resulted from the development of the industrial revolution, he found himself in hearty accord. Capitalism with its credit system, its banks and debt-funding and money manipulation, was wholly congenial to his masterful temperament. He read Adam Smith with eagerness and *The Wealth of Nations* was a source book for many of his state papers. To create in America an English system of finance, and an English system of industrialism, seemed to him the surest means to the great end he had in view; a centralizing capitalism would be more than a match for a decentralizing agrarianism, and the power of the state would augment with the increase of liquid wealth.

But granted that he lacked the intellectual qualities of the philosopher, it does not follow that his significance diminishes. On the contrary his very independence of contemporary European theory enlarged his serviceableness to party. He was free to employ his intelligence on the practical difficulties of a new and unprecedented situation. English liberalism did not answer the needs of Federalism, if indeed it could answer the needs of the country at large. The time had come to decide whether the long movement of decentralization should go further, and confirm the future government as a loose confederacy of powerful states, or whether an attempt should be made to check that movement and establish a counter tendency towards centralized, organized control. If the former, it meant surrendering the country to a democratic *laissez faire,* and there was nothing in the history of political *laissez faire* as it had developed in America, that justified the principle to Hamilton. It had culminated in agrarianism with legislative majorities riding down all obstacles, denying the validity of any check upon its will, constitutional, legal or ethical. The property interests of the minority had been rendered insecure. There had been altogether too much *laissez faire;* what was needed was sharp control of legislative majorities; the will of the majority must be held within due metes and bounds. Even in the economic world the principle of *laissez faire* no longer satisfied the needs of the situation. Parliamentary enactments had aided British interests in their exploitation of America before the war; it was only common sense for an American government to assist American business. The new capitalism that was rising stood in need of governmental subsidies. Business was languishing; infant industries could not compete on even terms with the powerful British manufacturing interests, long established and with ample capital. From a realistic contemplation of these facts Hamilton deduced the guiding principle that has since been followed, namely, that governmental interference with economic laws is desirable when it aids business, but intolerable and unsound when it aims at business regulation or control, or when it assists agriculture or labor.

Throughout his career Hamilton was surprisingly consistent. His mind hardened early as it matured early, and he never saw cause to challenge the principles which he first espoused. He was what a friendly critic would call a political realist, and an enemy would pronounce a cynic. With the practical man's contempt for theorists and idealists, he took his stand on current fact. He looked to the past for guidance, trusting to the wisdom of experience; those principles which have worked satisfactorily heretofore may be expected to work satisfac-

torily in the future. Whoever aspires to become a sane political leader must remember that his business is not to construct Utopias, but to govern men; and if he would succeed in that difficult undertaking he must be wise in the knowledge of human nature. At the basis of Hamilton's political philosophy was the traditional Tory psychology. Failure to understand human nature, he believed, was the fatal weakness of all democratic theorists; they put into men's breeches altruistic beings fitted only for a Utopian existence. But when we consider men as they are, we discover that they are little other than beasts, who if unrestrained will turn every garden into a pigsty. Everywhere men are impelled by the primitive lust of aggression, and the political philosopher must adjust his system to this unhappy fact. He must not suffer the charge of cynicism to emasculate his philosophy; "the goodness of government consists in a vigorous execution," rather than in amiable intentions; it is the business of the practical man and not of the theorist.

It needs no very extensive reading in Hamilton to discover ample justification for such an interpretation of his political philosophy; the evidence lies scattered broadly through his pages. At the precocious age of seventeen he laid down the thesis, "A vast majority of mankind is entirely biassed by motives of self-interest"; and as political systems are determined by the raw material of the mass of the people, they must be conditioned by such egoism. A year later he discovered in Hume the central principle of his philosophy:

Political writers, says a celebrated author, have established it as a maxim, that, in contriving any system of government, and fixing the several checks and controls of the constitution, *every man* ought to be supposed a *knave;* and to have no other end, in all his actions, but *private interest.* By this interest we must govern him; and, by means of it, *make him co-operate to public good,* notwithstanding his insatiable avarice and ambition. Without this, we shall in vain boast of the advantages of *any constitution.*[1]

At the age of twenty-seven he reiterated the doctrine, "The safest reliance of every government, is on men's interests. This is a principle of human nature, on which all political speculation, to be just, must be founded."[2] Obviously this was not a pose of youthful cynicism, but a sober judgment confirmed by observation and experience.

Accepting self-interest as the mainspring of human ambition, Hamilton accepted equally the principle of class domination. From his reading of history he discovered that the strong overcome the weak, and as they grasp power they coalesce into a master group. This master group will dominate, he believed, not only to further its interests, but to prevent the spread of anarchy which threatens every society split into factions and at the mercy of rival ambitions. In early days the master group was a military order, later it became a landed aristocracy, in modern times it is commercial; but always its power rests on property. "That power which holds the pursestrings absolutely, must rule," he stated unequivocally. The economic masters of society of necessity become the political masters. It is unthinkable that government should not reflect the wishes of property, that it should be permanently hostile to the greater economic interests; such hostility must destroy it, for no man or group of men will be ruled by those

whom they can buy and sell. And in destroying itself it will give place to another government, more wisely responsive to the master group; for even a democratic people soon learns that any government is better than a condition of anarchy, and a commercial people understands that a government which serves the interests of men of property, serves the interests of all, for if capital will not invest how shall labor find employment? And if the economic masters do not organize society efficiently, how shall the common people escape ruin?

Such are the fundamental principles which lie at the base of Hamilton's philosophy. He was in accord with John Adams and James Madison and Noah Webster, in asserting the economic basis of government, with its corollary of the class struggle. He not only accepted the rule of property as inevitable, but as desirable. As an aristocrat he deliberately allied himself with the wealthy. That men divide into the rich and the poor, the wise and the foolish, he regarded as a commonplace too evident to require argument. The explanation is to be sought in human nature and human capacities. For the common people, about whom Jefferson concerned himself with what seemed to Hamilton sheer demagoguery, he felt only contempt. Their virtues and capacities he had no faith in. "I am not much attached to the *majesty of the multitude,*" he said during the debate over the Constitution, "and waive all pretensions (founded on such conduct) to their countenance." His notorious comment — which the American democrat has never forgiven him, "The people! — the people is a great beast!" — was characteristically frank. Hamilton was no demagogue and nothing was plainer to his logic than the proposition that if the people possessed the capacity

[1] *Works,* Vol. II, p. 51.

[2] *Ibid.,* p. 298.

to rule, their weight of numbers would give them easy mastery; whereas their yielding to the domination of the gifted few proves their incapacity. A wise statesman, therefore, will consider the people no further than to determine how government may be least disturbed by their factional discontent, and kept free to pursue a logical program. Under a republican form good government is difficult to maintain, but not impossible. The people are easily deceived and turned aside from their purpose; like children they are diverted by toys; but if they become unruly they must be punished. Too much is at stake in government for them to be permitted to muddle policies.

It is sufficiently clear that in tastes and convictions Hamilton was a high Tory. The past to which he appealed was a Tory past, the psychology which he accepted was a Tory psychology, the law and order which he desired was a Tory law and order. His philosophy was not liked by republican America, and he knew that it was not liked. Practical business men accepted both his premises and conclusions, but republicans under the spell of revolutionary idealism, and agrarians suffering in their pocketbooks, would oppose them vigorously. He was at pains, therefore, as a practical statesman, to dress his views in a garb more seemly to plebeian prejudices, and like earlier Tories he paraded an ethical justification for his Toryism. The current Federalist dogma of the divine right of justice — *vox justiciae vox dei* — was at hand to serve his purpose and he made free use of it. But no ethical gilding could quite conceal a certain ruthlessness of purpose; in practice justice became synonymous with expediency, and expediency was curiously like sheer Tory will to power.

In certain of his principles Hamilton was a follower of Hobbes. His philosophy conducted logically to the leviathan state, highly centralized, coercive, efficient. But he was no idealist to exalt the state as the divine repository of authority, an enduring entity apart from the individual citizen and above him. He regarded the state as a highly useful instrument, which in the name of law and order would serve the interests of the powerful, and restrain the turbulence of the disinherited. For in every government founded on coercion rather than good will, the perennial unrest of those who are coerced is a grave menace; in the end the exploited will turn fiercely upon the exploiters. In such governments, therefore, self-interest requires that social unrest shall be covered with opprobium and put down by the police power; and the sufficient test of a strong state lies in its ability to protect the privileges of the minority against the anarchy of the majority. In his eloquent declamation against anarchy Hamilton was a conspicuous disciple of the law and order school. From the grave difficulties of post-Revolutionary times with their agrarian programs, he created a partisan argument for a leviathan state, which fell upon willing ears; and in the Constitutional convention, which, more than any other man, he was instrumental in assembling, he was the outstanding advocate of the coercive state.

In his plan of government presented to the Convention, the principle of centralized power was carried further than most would go, and his supporting speeches expressed doctrines that startled certain of his hearers. He was frankly a monarchist, and he urged the monarchical principle with Hobbesian logic. "The principle chiefly intended to be established is this — that there must be a permanent *will*." "There ought to be a principle in government capable of resisting the popular current."

Gentlemen say we need to be rescued from the democracy. But what [are] the means proposed? A democratic assembly is to be checked by a democratic senate, and both these by a democratic chief magistrate. The end will not be answered, the means will not be equal to the object. It will, therefore, be feeble and inefficient.[3]

The only effective way of keeping democratic factionalism within bounds, Hamilton was convinced, lay in the erection of a powerful chief magistrate, who "ought to be hereditary, and to have so much power, that it will not be his interest to risk much to acquire more," and who would therefore stand "above corruption." Failing to secure the acceptance of the monarchical principle, he devoted himself to the business of providing all possible checks upon the power of the democracy. He "acknowledged himself not to think favorably of republican government; but he addressed his remarks to those who did think favorably of it, in order to prevail on them to tone their government as high as possible."[4] His argument was characteristic:

All communities divide themselves into the few and the many. The first are the rich and well born, the other the mass of the people. The voice of the people has been said to be the voice of God; and, however generally this maxim has been quoted and believed, it is not true to fact. The people are turbulent and changing; they seldom judge or determine

right. Give, therefore, to the first class a distinct, permanent share in the government. They will check the unsteadiness of the second; and as they cannot receive any advantage by a change, they therefore will ever maintain good government. Can a democratic assembly, who annually revolve in the mass of the people, be supposed steadily to pursue the public good? Nothing but a permanent body can check the imprudence of democracy. Their turbulent and uncontrollable disposition requires checks.[5]

The argument scarcely needs refuting today, although curiously enough, it was rarely questioned by eighteenth-century gentlemen. It was the stock in trade of the Federalists, nevertheless Hamilton was too acute a thinker not to see its fallacy. It denied the fundamental premise of his political philosophy. If men are actuated by self-interest, how does it come about that this sovereign motive abdicates its rule among the rich and well born? Is there a magic in property that regenerates human nature? Do the wealthy betray no desire for greater power? Do the strong and powerful care more for good government than for class interests? Hamilton was fond of appealing to the teaching of experience; but he had read history to little purpose if he believed such notions. How mercilessly he would have exposed the fallacy in the mouth of Jefferson! It was a class appeal, and he knew that it was a class appeal, just as he knew that success knows no ethics. He was confronted by a situation in practical politics, and in playing ignobly upon selfish fears he was seeking to force the convention towards the English model. He had no confidence in the Constitution as finally adopted, and spoke in contemptuous terms of its weakness;

[3] Brief of speech submitting his plan of Constitution, in *Works*, Vol. II, p. 415.

[4] *Elliot's Debates*, Vol. V, p. 244.

[5] *Ibid.*, Vol. I, p. 422.

whereas for the British constitution he
had only praise, going so far, according
to Jefferson, as to defend the notorious
corruption of parliament on the ground
of expediency: "purge it of its corruption"— Jefferson reports him as saying —
"and give to its popular branch equality
of representation, and it would become
an *impracticable* government; as it stands
at present, with all its supposed defects,
it is the most perfect government which
ever existed."[6] The argument savors of
cynicism, but it is in keeping with his
philosophy; the British constitution owed
its excellence to the fact that in the name
of the people it yielded control of the
state to the landed aristocracy.

It was as a statesman that the brilliant
qualities of Hamilton showed to fullest
advantage. In developing his policies as
Secretary of the Treasury he applied his
favorite principle, that government and
property must join in a close working
alliance. The new government would remain weak and ineffective so long as it
was hostile to capital; but let it show itself friendly to capital, and capital would
make haste to uphold the hands of government. Confidence was necessary to
both, and it was a plant of slow growth,
sensitive to cold winds. The key to the
problem lay in the public finance, and
the key to a strong system of finance lay
in a great national bank. This, Hamilton's
dearest project, was inspired by the example of the Bank of England. No other
institution would so surely link the great
merchants to government, he pointed
out, for by being made partners in the
undertaking they would share both the
responsibility and the profits. It was notorious that during the Revolution men
of wealth had forced down the continental currency for speculative purposes;
was it not as certain that they would
support an issue in which they were

6 *Works of Jefferson*, Ford edition, Vol. I, p. 165.

interested? The private resources of
wealthy citizens would thus become an
asset of government, for the bank would
link "the interest of the State in an intimate connection with those of the rich
individuals belonging to it." "The men
of property in America are enlightened
about their own interest, and would easily be brought to see the advantage of
a good plan." Hence would arise stability
and vigor of government.

Moreover, the bank would be of immense service in the pressing business of
the public debt. In regard to this difficult
matter Hamilton was early convinced
that only one solution was possible: all
outstanding obligations, state and national, must be assumed by the Federal
government at face value, and funded.
Anything short of that would amount to
repudiation of a lawful contract, entered
into in good faith by the purchaser; and
such repudiation would destroy in the
minds of the wealthy the confidence in
the integrity of the new government that
was vital to its success. It was true that
speculators would reap great and unearned profits; but the speculators for
the most part were the principal men of
property whose support was so essential
that any terms were justifiable, and
nothing would bind them so closely to
the government as the knowledge that it
would deal generously with them. It was
true also that thousands of small men
would lose by such a transaction; but
under any existing social economy the
small man was at a disadvantage, and the
present state of affairs was not such as to
justify Utopian measures. To alienate the
rich and powerful in order to conciliate
the poor and inconsequential seemed to
him sheer folly. The argument of expediency must prevail over abstract justice;
the government must make terms with
those in whose hands lay the success or
failure of the venture.

His report on the public credit, of January 14, 1790, is one of the significant documents in the history of American finance. It is the first elaboration by an American statesman of the new system of capitalization and credit developed in eighteenth-century England, and it laid a broad foundation for later capitalistic development. To less daring financiers of the time the public debt was no more than a heavy obligation to be met; but to Hamilton it offered an opportunity for revivifying the whole financial life of the nation. Let the debts be consolidated and capitalized by a proper system of funding, and the augmented credit would multiply capital, lower the rate of interest, increase land values, and extend its benefits through all lines of industry and commerce. It was a bold plan and it encountered bitter opposition, which was not lessened by the heavy taxation that it called for. In his tax proposals Hamilton revealed his political philosophy so nakedly as almost to prove his undoing. His doctrine of the blessing of a national debt smacked rather too strongly of English Toryism for the American stomach.

A national debt, if it be not excessive, will be to us a national blessing. It will be a powerful cement to our Union. It will also create a necessity for keeping up taxation to a degree which, without being oppressive, will be a spur to industry. . . . It were otherwise to be feared our popular maxims would incline us to too great parsimony and indulgence. We labor less now than any civilized nation of Europe; and a habit of labor in the people, is as essential to the health and vigor of their minds and bodies, as it is conducive to the welfare of the State.[7]

A further struggle was encountered over the proposals of an internal revenue and a tariff. In his advocacy of the former Hamilton encountered the vigorous opposition of the backcountry. The total lack of adequate means of transportation rendered the problem of a grain market a chronic difficulty to the frontier farmers. The most convenient solution lay in distilling, and so whisky had become the chief commodity of the farmer that was transportable and brought a cash price. In placing a tax upon distilled liquors, therefore, Hamilton struck so directly at the economic interests of thousands of backwoodsmen, as to bring a rebellion upon the new administration. He knew what he was doing, but he calculated that it was safer to incur the enmity of farmers than of financiers; nevertheless the fierceness of the opposition surprised him, and aroused all the ruthlessness that lay in the background of his nature. He called for the strong arm of the military and when the rising was put down, he was angered at Washington's leniency in refusing to hang the convicted leaders. In his advocacy of a tariff he was on safer ground, for he was proposing a solution of the difficult situation confronting the manufacturers. Something must be done to revive industry so long stagnant. The old colonial machinery had been destroyed and new machinery must be provided. Industrial independence must follow political independence; and the easiest way lay in providing a tariff barrier behind which the infant industries of America might grow and become sufficient for domestic needs.

In his notable report on manufactures, submitted on December 5, 1791, Hamilton showed his characteristic intelligence in his grasp of the principles of the industrial revolution. Certainly no other man in America saw so clearly the significance of the change that was taking place in English industrialism, and what tremendous reservoirs of wealth the new order laid open to the country that tapped them. The productive possibili-

[7] *Works*, Vol. I, p. 257.

ties that lay in the division of labor, factory organization, the substitution of the machine for the tool, appealed to his materialistic imagination, and he threw himself heart and soul into the cause of industrial development in America. He accepted frankly the principle of exploitation. He was convinced that the interests of the manufacturers were one with the national interests, and he proposed to put the paternal power of the government behind them. With the larger social effects — the consequences to the working classes, congestion of population, the certainty of a labor problem — he concerned himself no more than did contemporary English statesmen. He was contemptuous of Jefferson's concern over such things. He had no Physiocratic leanings towards agriculture; material greatness alone appealed to him; and he contemplated with satisfaction the increase in national wealth that would accrue from levying toll upon the weak and helpless.

Besides this advantage of occasional employment to classes having different occupations, there is another, of a nature allied to it, and of a similar tendency. This is the employment of persons who would otherwise be idle, and in many cases, a burthen on the community, either from bias of temper, habit, infirmity of body, or some other cause, indisposing or disqualifying them for the toils of the country. It is worthy of particular remark, that, in general, women and children are rendered more useful, and the latter more early useful, by manufacturing establishments, than they would otherwise be. Of the number of persons employed in the cotton manufactories of Great Britain, it is computed that four-sevenths, nearly, are women and children; of whom the greatest propor-

tion are children, and many of them of a tender age.[8]

If the material power and splendor of the state be the great end of statesmanship — as Hamilton believed — no just complaint can be lodged against such a policy; but if the well-being of the individual citizen be the chief end — as Jefferson maintained — a very different judgment must be returned.

Although the fame of Hamilton has been most closely associated with the principle of constitutional centralization, his truer significance is to be found in his relation to the early developments of our modern capitalistic order. In his understanding of credit finance and the factory economy, he grasped the meaning of the economic revolution which was to transform America from an agrarian to an industrial country; and in urging the government to further such development, he blazed the path that America has since followed. "A very great man," Woodrow Wilson has called him, "but not a great American." In the larger historical meaning of the term, in its democratic implications, that judgment is true; but in the light of our industrial history, with its corporate development and governmental subsidies, it does not seem so true. As the creative organizer of a political state answering the needs of a capitalistic order — a state destined to grow stronger as imperialistic ambitions mount — he seems the most modern and the most American of our eighteenth-century leaders, one to whom our industrialism owes a very great debt, but from whom our democratic liberalism has received nothing.

[8] *Works,* Vol. III, pp. 207–208.

Suggestions for Additional Reading

The readings in this volume provide only a few samples of the controversy which raged at the time of the adoption of the funding system. Much additional material is available. For the complete record of the debates in the House of Representatives (so far as they exist) the student should of course consult the *Annals of Congress*. Hamilton's most important state papers on finance have been often reproduced and can easily be located in unabridged form, among other places, in both the *American State Papers, Finance*, Vol. 1, and in the *Annals of Congress*, Gales and Seaton edition, Vols. 2 and 3. A detailed reproduction of his writings on finance, including not only state papers but also important letters and unofficial writings, may be found in Henry Cabot Lodge, ed., *The Works of Alexander Hamilton* (9 vols., New York: 1885), II. Of special interest in this volume of Lodge's *Works* are Hamilton's defense of the funding system (reproduced only in part in the preceding pages) which appears in "Objections and Answers Respecting the Administration of the Government," pp. 237–279, and "Vindication of the Funding System," pp. 285–305.

Brief but highly enlightening comments on the issues involved may be discovered among the papers of most of the leading statesmen of the time. For the Federalist point of view, those of Fisher Ames, Rufus King, and Oliver Wolcott may be noted, and for the anti-Federalist viewpoint, those of William Maclay and Thomas Jefferson. The lat-

ter's views are briefly summarized in *The Anas* (Vol. IX, Book III, Part V of H. A. Washington, ed., *The Writings of Thomas Jefferson*, Washington, D.C., 1854, 9 vols.), 91–96.

In addition, the partisan strife over the funding issue gave rise to controversial pamphlets and bred bitter newspaper controversies. These materials are not usually available except in large university libraries, but the student who has such a resource at his command will find helpful references to this literature in Charles A. Beard, *Economic Origins of Jeffersonian Democracy* (New York, 1927), especially pages 196 and 221, and Joseph Dorfman, *The Economic Mind in American Civilization 1606–1865* (New York, 1946, 3 vols.), Chapter XIII. Especially to be noted are the writings of John Taylor of Caroline, who most forcefully presented the philosophy of the southern opposition to Hamilton's system in his pamphlets, *An Examination of the Late Proceedings in Congress Respecting the Official Conduct of the Secretary of the Treasury* (1793), and *Inquiry into the Principles and Tendencies of Certain Public Measures* (1794).

Many biographies of Hamilton have been written but though all pay tribute to his financial genius, few add much to an understanding of the merits of his program for funding the debt. Of the older books those most useful are John T. Morse, Jr., *The Life of Alexander Hamilton* (2 vols., Boston, 1876), I, Chapters VII–XII, and William Graham Sumner, *Alexander Hamilton* (New York, 1890),

Chapters X–XIII. Of more recent biographies, one of the best is Nathan Schachner, *Alexander Hamilton* (New York, 1946), Chapters XVII–XXII. Excellent for its presentation of background material as well as its dramatic, pro-Jefferson account of the struggle between the two leaders is Claude G. Bowers, *Jefferson and Hamilton, The Struggle for Democracy in America* (Boston, 1925).

Most of the biographies of Hamilton present a more or less favorable picture of his financial policies. Supplementing these is Albert S. Bolles, *The Financial History of the United States from 1789 to 1860* (New York, 1883). His first eleven chapters in Book I provide a detailed description of the public finance of the period and Chapter IX gives an extremely favorable evaluation of Hamilton's administration of the treasury. Also worth attention is the unusual defense of Hamilton's policies briefly made by

Morris Zucker, *The Philosophy of American History, Periods in American History* (New York, 1945), pp. 325–332. For interpretations, on the whole critical, of Hamilton's policies, the books by Beard and Bowers already referred to should be consulted. Finally, the student may wish to read the accounts of this controversy in some of the major histories of the United States and to compare their varying shades of interpretation. Though others might well be included, the following provide an interesting sampling: Richard Hildreth, *The History of the United States of America* (6 vols., New York, 1851), IV; James Schouler, *History of the United States of America* (7 vols., New York, 1894), I; John Bach McMaster, *A History of the People of the United States* (8 vols., New York, 1883), I; and Edward Channing, *A History of the United States* (6 vols., New York, 1927), IV.